COMMUNITY CONFLICT&THE PRESS

———————— **PEOPLE AND COMMUNICATION** ————————

Series Editors: PETER CLARKE   *University of Michigan*
                    F. GERALD KLINE *University of Minnesota*

Volumes in this series:

Phillip J. **TICHENOR** George A. **DONOHUE** Clarice N. **OLIEN**

COMMUNITY CONFLICT&THE
PRESS

Introduction by PETER CLARKE

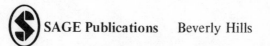 **SAGE Publications** Beverly Hills London

For information address:

SAGE Publications, Inc.
275 South Beverly Drive
Beverly Hills, California 90212

SAGE Publications Ltd
28 Banner Street
London EC1Y 8QE, England

Printed in the United States of America

Library of Congress Cataloging in Publication Data

Tichenor, Phillip J
    Mass communication, policy, and community conflict.

    (People and communication ; 8)
    Includes bibliographies.
    1. Mass media--Political aspects--Minnesota.
2. Public opinion--Minnesota. 3. Pluralism (Social sciences) 4. Social conflict. I. Donohue, George, joint author. II. Olien, Clarice, joint author.
III. Title.
HN79.M63M37   301.16'1'09776   79-24401
ISBN 0-8039-1425-3
ISBN 0-8039-1426-1 pbk.

FIRST PRINTING

CONTENTS

Series Editor's Introduction

In this volume the authors push ahead with their continuing study of links between community structure and roles of the press.[1] Their work lies within a tradition viewing mass communication as an organic part of larger social systems, composed of publics relating to elites through acquiescence or participation. Although this analytic tradition is strong,[2] empirical evidence clarifying press roles has been disappointingly scarce.

While digesting the findings reported in this volume, readers may wish to review the significance of pluralism as a structural feature. Consideration of its communicative significance instantly affirms that pluralism means more than size of place.[3] Pluralistic communities are marked by competition among elites in the allocation of valued resources. They offer many opportunities for satisfying economic needs, for socializing, for learning and personal development, for religious experience, for altruism and helping others, for being entertained, and for the array of other values people express. The Yellow Pages of the telephone directory contain simple and vivid indexes of diversity; census records, including mobility patterns, complete the picture.

Pluralistic communities need a mass media system to become alerted to conflict in resource allocation and to observe how disagreements are settled. In such places the distribution of information often affects conflict resolution as much as allegiance to elites. Where people act in different ways, adhering to varying beliefs, the press can publicize the alternatives through its selection of news sources.

Whether mass media fulfill these opportunities is a matter for empirical test. The outcome is bound to depend on the division of labor one finds within communication systems, as well as pluralism in community structure.

Appropriately, Tichenor, Donohue, and Olien's findings are built upon communities as the units of analysis. Issues in the news are studied that pit local people against external forces. Perceived roles of the press as well as the links between conflict and press coverage are examined. The authors conclude by focusing on communication and the "knowledge gap."

These data suggest a frame within which qualitative judgments about press performance can be conducted. Pluralism, resources enjoyed by the press, and the importance of issue outcomes set boundaries within which journalistic efforts will vary. Research into the intensity of political election coverage provides ample evidence of this variance, noting the effort reporters and editors expend—frequency of interviewing, reading documents, prying, cross-checking, attending important meetings, and the like.[4] Hard work translates into media coverage. Where resourcefulness in informing the public is encouraged, we can expect understanding and processes of conflict resolution to benefit, especially in pluralistic settings. Where effort goes unrewarded, decision processes wither or are monopolized by an interlocking directorate.

Judgments about a news medium should rest on its over- or underachievement, comparing it to norms for communities of equal pluralism. We should value initiative by a small town paper more highly than equal exertion in a less homogeneous environment. Where informing faces barriers, performance wins special praise.

The following chapters skirt evaluative judgments and rightly so. But analysis and discussion should help teachers of communication ethics as surely as these pages inform our understanding of mass media within social systems.

This is one study in which data contain both normative and sociological implications.

—Peter Clarke

NOTES

1. See their earlier report in Peter Clarke (ed.) *New Models for Communication Research* (Beverly Hills: SAGE, 1973).

2. Hanno Hardt, *Social Theories of the Press* (Beverly Hills: SAGE, 1979).

3. Michael A. DuBick, "The Organizational Structure of Newspapers in Relation to their Metropolitan Environments," *Administrative Science Quarterly*, 23:418-433 (1978).

4. Peter Clarke and Susan H. Evans, "Campaign reporting by the press: autonomy in the newsroom and election coverage," presented at the meeting of the American Sociological Association, Boston, August 1979.

1

Communication and Community Conflict

There is a deeply ingrained belief among scholars and the general public that in a participatory democracy, citizens should be encouraged to acquire as much information about public decisions as possible. It is further assumed that acquisition of information will supposedly result in the best decision on an issue. Reaching this decision may be thwarted by the low level of information which, as evidence indicates, citizens often possess even about topics central to their collective and individual self interests.

While it is not clear that more information among more people would lead to the most desirable decisions, it is quite clear that possession of information, or access to it, is a potentially crucial resource for the power position of groups that are seeking to realize or protect their collective interests.

This book considers how information is generated and communicated to various publics in modern communities and how characteristics of community structure and conflict come to bear on communication processes. Data relating to these propositions have been gathered from field studies in 19 different communities in Minnesota. The analysis addresses what people know, how they find out, and what they think about questions

AUTHORS' NOTE: We wish to acknowledge support for this research from the University of Minnesota Agricultural Experiment Station and Agricultural Extension Service.

that frequently strike at community survival and continuation of a way of life.

The communities studied vary in size from rural places under 2,000 population to suburban communities and urban centers as large as 100,000. The study does not include large metropolitan complexes as wholes, although it does include suburban and metropolitan fringe areas. Size and structure of the community are seen as major characteristics affecting newspapers and their impact on the course of a controversy.

COMMUNITY AND LARGER SOCIETY

Situations studied in the 19 communities represent issues which often receive wide attention. These issues include:

(1) locating a nuclear power plant in a small town amid questions of safety and radioactive fallout

(2) communities struggling with the question of regional political organization and development

(3) three communities trying to resolve sewage disposal problems in compliance with state water quality and antipollution regulations

(4) environmentalist pressure leading to legal moves to stop a taconite plant from discharging waste into a lake

(5) court challenges of mining and logging in a wilderness area

(6) closing a steel mill that was a city's major employer, following years of public discussion about plant obsolescence and air quality standards which the plant could not meet

(7) angry and organized farmers, with the support of a city council, opposing establishment of a high-voltage power line supported by 150-foot-high towers across county farmland.

While differing in topic and technical detail, all of the above issues illustrate an increasingly apparent condition of social change: American communities, large and small, are finding themselves with shrinking power to control their own destinies. It is difficult to mention a single major community decision today that is not affected in some decisive way by forces external to the community itself. Urban renewal is a well-known case in point; large federal grants are brought in to alter buildings, sanitary facilities, and other features of the physical and social landscape. Housing development projects depend heavily on federal aid, as do school improvement, community health programs, and a variety of social services. With aid comes an increasing amount of control from centralized authority, at the state or national level or both.

However, the force of external agencies is not confined to the public sector. The entire retail establishment of the typical community has evolved from a series of individually and locally owned entrepreneurial operations to a retail system often dominated by franchise arrangements. The familiar trademarks of discount stores, fast food outlets, and industries appear along with personnel and managerial control from beyond the local area.

Such external involvement in the community, while historically a potential source of controversy, is relatively unquestioned as long as the involvement is seen as something the community requested. Powers of external agencies take on a new social dimension, however, when public and private agencies initiate actions and projects regardless of, and sometimes in spite of, the wishes of the host community. A wide range of facilities and programs impinging on communities have been developed at the state and national levels since World War II. Such programs have been justified by that part of our credo which obliges a small portion of individuals and citizens to sustain a certain amount of hardship for the greater societal good. Environmental restrictions, siting of nuclear power plants and use of eminent domain for utilities, highways, and parks are contemporary examples. Energy program decisions are increasingly of this type, with either utilities or state agencies making decisions about locating generating plants or power lines in areas where they may have severe local consequences but are deemed necessary to provide energy for society as a whole. As Coleman (1957) has put it, problems are frequently "laid at the community's doorstep." Now, a particular *solution* is often laid at the doorstep, bearing the imprint of "general welfare."

Consequences of acts by external agencies may have been less apparent two or three decades ago when community issues included fluoridation of water supplies and consolidation of rural and town schools. Such problems were often seen as having a local origin, with passage of state laws requiring fluoridation and consolidation generally regarded as facilitating a socially acceptable resolution. When individual communities cannot resolve the issue, the reasoning goes, *transfer* the decision-making function to a higher political level. Therefore, given the growing interdependence of communities and institutions and the history of state and federal legislation in dealing with previous controversies, one would predict that attempts at resolution of new and complex issues will lean heavily on state or federal legislation. The environmental movement, the women's rights movement, and the medicare-medicaid movements all concentrated on state and federal legislation. This trend toward greater centralization of decision making has affected most institutional areas.

Growing centralization of decision making may be a result of the nature of *problems* that go beyond local boundaries, the nature of *solutions* that go beyond local boundaries, or a combination of the two. Both factors and their combination tend to accelerate the trend toward centralization, so that local autonomy is becoming a nostalgic concept. Through the social technology of centralized decision making and program development, communities are increasingly locked into processes that they are often powerless to alter, and these constraints will continue until or unless the definition or the solution of the problem is conceptualized as having definite local inputs. The state and federal legislation is no longer seen as "enabling" or facilitating but rather as contracting and determining.

WHERE DOES INFORMATION COME FROM?

While the need for greater citizen understanding of issues may be generally agreed upon, ways of creating that understanding are not. There is, on the one hand, the traditional belief that responsible concerned citizens will inform themselves

(Hennessy, 1975). Parallel with that view is the belief that information media such as newspapers, broadcast stations, and educational institutions have a responsibility and should provide the needed knowledge. The view that individual citizens should bear the *sole* responsibility for finding out about issues is not viable, especially when the information and the system for dissemination within the community may be inadequate or nonexistent. As society becomes more diverse and complex, there is a growing expectation that the information agencies, particularly the mass media, will deliver information and interpretations through the use of experts and news analysis.

Growing diversity in society has been mirrored in the information delivery system, with increased use of such techniques as specialized sections of modern newspapers which appeal singly and in combination to different groups. Rapid growth of specialized magazines and publications targeted to limited and specific audiences also reflects this diversity. The rising importance of the "purposive communicator," (Westley and Mac-Lean, 1957) or advocate for a special interest group which seeks the attention of wider audiences through mass media channels, further suggests a system of social organization based on pluralistic special interest groups. The increasing number of purposive communicators (such as educators, public information and public relations specialists, and advertisers) illustrates not only the increased number of special interest groups but also the interdependence of groups attempting to control both generation and dissemination of knowledge.

A large portion of the information available, then, depends on an information delivery system which reflects the pluralistic organization and vested interests of the society in which it exists. Information appears to be generated and disseminated as a result of joint activity of professionals within the mass media channels and professionals who have advocacy functions for interdependent special interest groups. These professionals represent a form of system linkage and act as an interface among the groups.

PLURALISM AND MEDIA USE

Social environments of people are determined by the nature of the communities in which they live, work, and interact with others. Work opportunities, commercial centers, leisure time facilities, and public services may differ sharply according to size of the community, its location, and the way it is structured on other dimensions. It follows that availability of information about the public life of the community may vary according to the same characteristics. Will citizens of an isolated rural community, for example, have the same information environment as citizens of an urban center? If not, how will that environment differ? And what are some of the consequences?

While community structure may be characterized in several ways, a basic factor is the degree of pluralism—defined as the degree of differentiation in the social system along institutional and specialized interest group lines, in a way that determines the potential sources of organized social power. Previous research by Olien, Donohue, and Tichenor (1978) has generated support for the hypothesis that the less pluralistic the community, the more likely it is to be served by a weekly newspaper than by a daily, and the less likely the citizens are to use newspaper sources generally for keeping up with events and issues. The less pluralistic the community, the more likely citizens are to use and prefer television as a source of news and information (Westley and Severin, 1963). As communities become larger and more pluralistic, they are more likely to be served by daily newspapers and contrary tendencies should occur, with citizens using newspaper sources to a greater extent and depending upon television news less.

Given the marked differences in content among daily newspapers, weekly newspapers, and television, documentation of citizens' information environments is important in these different community situations. If the proposition is valid that the potential for citizen participation is related to the information available, these differences may have a variety of outcomes affecting the ability of citizens to make decisions concerning their individual and collective welfare.

NEWSPAPERS AND COMMUNITY CONTROVERSY

The role of newspapers and other mass media in community conflict is often recognized, and frequently the media are charged with creating the conflicts. They may be accused of "sensationalizing" and "blowing things out of proportion" or of "covering up" and "not paying attention to all sides" of a controversy (Gerald, 1963; Rivers and Schramm, 1969). Members of the media profession often answer the first accusation by saying that bringing things into the open is a necessary contribution to democratic processes (Small, 1970); the second criticism may be answered by the argument that newspapers are not simply conduits but must themselves make judgments about selection and presentation of news if they are to meet their professional obligations to the community in a responsible manner (Hulteng, 1976). In doing so, media professionals may argue, they must decide how much and what kind of play to give each side, risking the possibility that both sides may believe that their views have been underrepresented in the press.

Social conflict is a principal ingredient of much newspaper content since conflict is a central component in community life and social change. Differing interests and competing goals in a complex society lead to a variety of tensions which, themselves, create pressure for change. The pervasive nature of conflict has been pointed out by many writers (Dahrendorf, 1959; Coser, 1956, 1967). Marceau (1972) contends that in modernization programs entailing mass communication, messages to the public "become entangled" in the conflicts at the local level.

While writers such as Marceau tend to view conflict as a negative condition in communication, conflict may be viewed as either positive *or* negative. We also make the assumption that conflict may be a necessary process for mass diffusion of information, but not a sufficient condition. Conflict, then, is not necessarily a negative factor in communication, and this perspective has many practical ramifications for the distribution of information through newspapers and other mass media.

Several writers, representing the social conflict school of thought, have pointed to the role of conflict in arousing and maintaining citizen participation (Coser, 1956; Dahrendorf, 1959; Simmel, 1955). In a later work, Coser (1967) pointed out that the clash of values and ideas between competing interests and groups may be a sign of vitality and creativity. Conflict *within* a system can lead to revitalization of old norms or emergence of new ones; conflict with an *external* group may, in addition, strengthen internal cohesion. All of these consequences imply an increase in various forms of communication, including communication through mass media.

Conflict is not an uncontrolled process. Social and political organization provides a variety of mechanisms for regulating conflict in the interest of general social control. Interest groups, labor unions, political parties, legal systems, arbitration agencies, city councils, and county boards are mechanisms for regulating and directing conflict to gain partisan and/or collective ends. But conflict regulation is not entirely, or even necessarily, a matter of conflict resolution or elimination of tension. Conflict may well be *created* in the interest of serving group ends or of maintaining the system. Counterculture groups have employed this principle, as have various groups of scientists advocating or opposing certain uses of technology (Primack and von Hippel, 1974). Conflict may be regulated by a variety of formal procedures, such as formalized labor negotiations. The open public hearing as a forum for airing public views and grievances is a conflict control mechanism. The newspaper or broadcast news program may function much the same way. Levels of tension and degree of open exchange will vary widely from topic to topic and community to community; that kind of variation is a principal element for study here. The question is the extent to which newspapers contribute to development and control of conflict and the way they help shape the public's definition of the issue. Does the newspaper *create* new issues, hence conflict, or does it serve to *accelerate, decelerate, clarify,* or *redefine* conflicts which relate to the confluence of social forces in the community?

Newspapers regularly engage in message transactions involving major institutions and central values of the community and larger society. One of the newspaper's primary functions is social control, which it performs through persistently drawing attention to the oughts and naughts that generally prevail as a condition of the existing systems. The newspaper performs these functions not by outright moralizing alone, although that may occur, but through a pattern of news selection in topic and source that often reinforces values by implication (Broder, 1977). Neither the newspaper nor the broadcast station is organized to create new ideas or proposals for community consideration. They are only rarely equipped or motivated to examine proposals from different sectors of the community in an evaluative or critical way, let alone create new proposals of their own. Fundamentally, the newspaper and community broadcast station deal with the ideas and initiatives of their sources.

A fundamental hypothesis, then, is that newspapers tend to serve ancillary rather than initiating roles in the development of community conflicts. Concerted social action requires a degree of planning, coordination, and organized activity beyond the staff and capabilities of the newspaper. The organizational processes of governmental agencies, city councils, and legislatures may be neither understood nor appreciated by the individual journalists who report them. It is not unusual to find editors and reporters highly critical, if not hostile, toward committee activity and organizational procedure which are at the core of social action in both public and private sectors.

But if newspapers and other media do not initiate action, from whence comes the belief that community projects may be impossible without the media? The answer in theory is that newspapers like most mass media draw attention to organized activity that is already under way. The power or lack of power of the press stems in large measure from its ability and need to be selective (within limits) in choosing what to accelerate and what to leave languishing. For every urban renewal or environmental project given newspaper publicity in a community, informed citizens can usually name scores of other projects that never gained attention in print or were ignored in broadcast reports. A big question is, "who has the power to be selected for attention by the mass media?"

It may seem contradictory to argue that newspapers deal regularly in conflict while hardly ever initiating it. But the contradiction fades when one realizes that newspapers are regular recipients of ideas and information from a myriad of organized sources. There is very real competition from parties in a conflict for media space and time; even so-called investigative reporting is often a matter of deciding which overtures from news sources to accept (Bethell, 1977). The ordinary front page of a newspaper contains few items that resulted from journalistic initiative alone. A large portion of material is published because someone with a vested interest in the subject brought it to the newspaper's attention. Sigal (1973) found, for example, that nearly 74% of the information channels for foreign and national news in a sample of New York *Times* and Washington *Post* editions were *other* than reporter "enterprise." Press conferences and press releases alone accounted for 42% of the news channels.

If it is true that newspapers choose and select under varying degrees of pressure from items brought in by others, it is equally true that newspapers live with the most intense conflicts of their communities. But by living with these conflicts, newspapers do not necessarily turn the conflicts into public issues. They may play these conflicts down or avoid them entirely as often occurs in small communities or they may give the conflicts sustained front page play as often happens in the metropolitan press. Part of the nature of the newspaper's decision or judgment is a result of the social structure in which the newspaper operates. The characteristic differences between the rural and urban press result from the differences in the newspaper's environment; the environment does not differ because of the newspaper. The content decisions, dependent as they are on community structure, constitute a pattern of information control that has far-reaching implications for what the community will hear about, think about, and talk about.

To say that media are engaged in information control is not to say that diabolical forces are necessarily at work. The potential for such forces is there, however, and may be exploited in certain instances. Information control is one aspect of all information activities, including the conduct of social conflict. Decisions about information are made daily, and growing social and political complexity of the milieu in which communities thrive or falter creates a potential for a wealth of information on diverse topics. It is never possible to transmit or reproduce all of the information available; some decision about what to publish will be made. What is called "news judgment," "censorship," or "publicity" is, in each case, a decision about information and therefore an act of control. There may well be thousands of journalists, officials, functionaries, and citizens who make information judgments without thinking about the consequences, but those decisions are control acts despite this lack of deliberate consciousness.

NEWSPAPERS, CONFLICT, AND KNOWLEDGE GAPS

There is the traditional viewpoint that resolution of social problems is related to inputs of information. Accordingly, if a system is sufficiently saturated with information, a general understanding of the topic will develop within the system. Once understanding is at hand, resolution is assumed to be at hand.

Behind that viewpoint are at least three assumptions. One is that information itself contributes to resolution of social problems. That assumption is not challenged here. Open for study and examination, however, are two additional assumptions. The first, based on the educational principle of repetition, is that a medium of communication, such as a newspaper, can through sheer redundancy raise the overall level of understanding in the community. The second is that higher levels of information input will lead to a general equalization of knowledge throughout the system. Hence, more effective decision making is assumed to occur.

Both of these assumptions have been brought into question by systematic studies. The first, that redundancy of newspaper reporting can increase levels of understanding, has been difficult to demonstrate in some studies of publicity campaigns (Hyman and Sheatsley, 1947; Star and Hughes, 1950), in which levels of understanding of issues changed little or not at all following media campaigns. The second assumption, that more information inputs lead to equalization of knowledge, is even more strongly questioned. Selective self-exposure to information has frequently been found to be related to level of education. Furthermore, data in recent years indicate that the problem is not so much one of increasing knowledge but, frequently, one of relative deprivation of knowledge. A gap in knowledge between segments within a total system is entirely possible, and since social power is in part based on knowledge, relative deprivation of knowledge may lead to relative deprivation of power (Tichenor, Donohue, and Olien, 1970; Rogers, 1974; Katzman, 1973).

Specifically, several studies have supported the hypothesis that as the flow of information into a social system increases, groups with higher levels of education often tend to acquire this information at a faster rate than those with lower levels of education. This higher rate of acquisition results from the different roles and positions of more highly educated segments in the social system. Groups with higher education have higher verbal skills and more media resources available to them. Educational training creates habits that include a higher rate of attention to certain kinds of media content, including public affairs, and a trained capacity for understanding and retaining that information. Similarly, more highly educated groups are trained to recognize the relevance of information for their particular position in the social structure and for maintenance of that position.

As a result of the differential rates of acquisition, gaps in knowledge between segments with different levels of education tend to increase rather than decrease. Knowledge of space research is an example; after several years of heavy media attention to space rocketry and satellites, the gap in knowledge about that research across educational levels was greater than it had been before the space research program began. Similarly, knowledge gaps widened over time for the smoking and cancer issue.

Many of the findings on knowledge of national issues support the knowledge gap hypothesis. But these findings raise a question of major theoretical and social significance: Under what conditions does it increase and under what conditions, if any, might this knowledge gap be reduced or eliminated? If such gaps widen as the flow of information to specialized groups is increased, then that tendency should be reduced as a public issue is made relevant to the plurality of the groups involved. There may be basic concerns in communities, but the key question may be the extent to which groups singly or in interaction succeed in *defining* the issue as one of basic concern.

Newspaper coverage may be more likely to equalize levels of understanding to the extent that it contributes to the intensity of conflict in a neighborhood. This stimulation may overcome — at least partially—some of the selective dissemination and selective self-exposure patterns that contribute to the widening of the knowledge gap on topics of specialized interest.

If indeed research data indicate that newspaper coverage may lead to increased controversy, which in turn increases equalization of knowledge, the implications may be disturbing. Among dominant community values, frequently, is a belief that calls for quick resolution of conflict, if not elimination of it in the first place. There is also the popular belief that "nobody learns anything in a controversy." The general proposition for study here holds quite the opposite, that controversy draws attention to information which (1) has a bearing on competition between interest groups and (2) potentially puts one group in a better power position as a result of having the information. Underlying this reasoning is the assumption that redistribution of social power among constituent groups is one of the most basic concerns in society generally. This is not to say that all or most groups are necessarily *seeking* a redistribution of power, but that any question of changing power relationships is of general concern and that conflict tends to raise precisely that question. A group seeking to maintain the status quo will be as concerned about redistribution as a group that considers itself deprived and therefore seeks a power realignment. As a result of these concerns, there is an increased likelihood in a conflict that citizens of all status levels will acquire information relevant to that conflict. While there may be limits, the implication would be that intense controversies may lead to greater realization of a general democratic ideal: the sharing of an equalized quantity of information about a situation by nearly everyone.

CITIZEN KNOWLEDGE, OPINIONS, AND ATTITUDES

Another popular belief is that information and attitudes favorable to a movement go together. A specific version of this belief is that citizens will favor and actively support environmental restriction on industry or on their own lifestyles in proportion to their awareness of the facts about damage to the environment from industry or current personal habits of citizens. An assumption here is that people either are altruistic or act according to "intelligent self interest" in the long run.

The evidence to date on this question, in the literature of the social and behavioral sciences, is mixed. A frequent finding is that people are highly selective, so that new information tends to be interpreted in terms of already existing attitudes and opinions (Berelson and Steiner, 1964). Such selectivity may be overcome to some extent by persuasive communications appealing to an "intelligent self-interest," which may under some conditions present new interpretations, if not changes in opinions.

The question has special relevance for community conflict situations. If alternative points of view are expressed, the likelihood increases that people will hear this information. Also, a conflict may increase the likelihood that selective attention and interpretation will occur. That is, an intense conflict makes group alignments and group interests especially salient, potentially alerting the audience to the way any information relates to those alignments and interests. Such selectivity may occur in response to mass media messages or to organized group discussions. If a group session is identified with one point of view in an intense situation, those persons with opposite tendencies would likely avoid the group or drop out to a greater extent than committed individuals. This tendency has been identified frequently in studies based on "balance" theory, or cognitive dissonance (Festinger, 1957).

COMMUNITY GROUPINGS AND ISSUES

Research questions such as those addressed above were studied in 19 communities, selected according to the potentially controversial nature of the issue involved and the probability that the issue would receive high media coverage in the future. Thus, it was possible to follow issues through various stages in a context which provided a vehicle for testing research hypotheses. Selections of communities were based on the demonstrable fact that some of the most intense controversies stem from the interdependent linkages between communities and the larger society of which they are part. Therefore, in every community selected, the potential social conflict was based partly, if not entirely, on actions or pressures by state or federal agencies or other forces external to the communities themselves.

Issues in the 19 communities fall into five groupings according to the nature of the issue. Briefly, these include:

(1) the nuclear power issue, studied in three communities adjacent to the area in which a nuclear power plant was located and about to begin generating electricity

(2) the mining and metal industry grouping, in which four communities in the same region were studied in terms of knowlege of and reaction to three situations in which local industry would potentially be affected by state and federal environmental regulations

(3) the political regionalization grouping, in which six communities were studied regarding local familiarity with, and reaction to, regional development centers resulting from a recent state law enabling creation of such centers

(4) the water quality grouping, in which four communities with sewage disposal and/or river and lake pollution problems were studied

(5) the power line grouping, in which two communities were studied where a high voltage power line was planned and would cross local farm and other residential land, requiring easements or condemnation following a lengthy hearing process.

These community groupings are described in more detail below.

Community Group 1: Nuclear Power Issue

Communities D, N, and P in Minnesota were studied in the spring of 1969. The issue for all three centered around a nuclear power plant which had been constructed recently in their midst. Principal questions concerned radiation emission standards for plant operation and whether ultimate control over these standards would rest with the state or with the federal government. Permissible levels of emission had been specified for the plant by the U.S. Atomic Energy Commission several months earlier. In the two months preceding the studies in these communities, local and statewide media attention had focused on the power company and on activities of a voluntary organization which raised questions about possible release of radioactive wastes from the plant and their potential environmental effects. Interest in the problem heightened when, a few days before the field interviewing began, the Minnesota Pollution Control Agency issued a permit stating that total radiation could not exceed 2% of the federal standards. For the communities studied, the issue could be seen as a potential threat of radioactive fallout, or outside pressure against a local electrical generating industry, or both. There was also the general question of the need for electricity, although this was some three years before the energy crisis became an issue in the fall of 1973. Thus, the question of possible energy shortages if the project were not approved got very little attention. The latter illustrates the role of problem definition and the nature of information relevancy. The three communities studied are located in a roughly sequential geographic order, with the power plant in the center community which is a section of a rural county. The other two communities are a city of about 30,000 at one end of the rural county and a metropolitan suburban community on the other.

Community Group 2: Mining and Metal Industry Issues

Issues in these communities were air pollution by a steel plant in community C, taconite tailings discharged into a lake community J, and mining exploration in a federally designated recreation area in community L.

The steel plant had been community C's largest employer in the 1960s. State and federal pollution control agencies applied pressure to the plant in the late 1960s to meet air pollution standards. A basic local issue was whether the company could meet these standards without reducing or discontinuing operations. The issue received continued publicity and statewide political attention for the next two years, during which major developments occurred. Legislation to provide tax concessions if the plant would modernize was considered but rejected by the state legislature in 1971. In the summer of that year, the company began closing part of its operations, cutting its total employment from 2,500 to under 1,000. In January of 1972, the governor appointed a special committee to consider unemployment in the area, amid speculation that this panel would also consider tax concessions to the steel plant if it would modernize. Such arrangements were not made, and by the end of 1972 most of the plant's operations had been suspended.

In community J the issue concerned a taconite processing plant that provides more than two-thirds of the jobs in a community of under 4,000 population. The question in the early 1970s was whether tailings, which the plant discharges into a large lake, would have harmful effects on that body of water; community C gets its drinking water from that same lake. There were contradictory opinions about the effect of the tailings from different scientists, and testimony from both sides had received some publicity. Statewide publicity early in the period made it clear that survival of community J was at stake and could depend on how strictly antipollution standards were enforced. It was frequently presented as a question of allowing the plant to operate as usual or forcing it to stop the discharge, closing the plant and bringing economic disaster to the town. The issue continued to be an intense legal controversy for at least seven years, with state and federal agencies making several legal moves to halt the release of the tailings into the lake. The question had not been resolved at the time of the survey upon which analysis is based.

In community L, there was a general issue that involved questions of exploration for mining in a federal recreation area, mining itself in nearby areas, and commercial logging in the recreation area. In each case, local groups seeking increased employment and economic development supported the proposed activity, while environmental agencies and local groups concerned about the recreation aspects of the area opposed it. The community is one of several in Minnesota that a half century ago had a brisk mining activity but has since seen most of its nearby mines close. The question of mining in the recreation area itself was eventually resolved in 1973 by a court order banning such mining, but the related question of mining in other areas and logging in the recreation area has received regional and statewide publicity since 1971.

In at least two of these issues, taconite and the mining-logging question, public debate frequently took on an acrimonious tone of rural community versus metropolitan city. The environmental groups, many of whom had headquarters and large memberships in the metropolitan area, advocated cessation of tailing discharge in the lake and banning of mining and logging. These groups were attacked publicly by spokespersons for the two rural communities. These attacks frequently characterized the environmental groups as highly urban—which was at least partially correct in terms of membership and entirely correct in terms of where the environmental groups were based. A statement often made by community leaders was that "environmentalism means protecting summer playgrounds for the big city vacationers," without being concerned about the local economy and survival of small rural communities. None of these issues was immediately relevant in community H, which is in the same general area of the state and was selected as a comparison community. Community C is the largest city in the study, a diversified urban center of more than 100,000 population. Communities L and J are both under 5,000, and community H had a population of slightly less than 3,000 at the time of the study.

Community Group 3: Political Regionalization

In communities A, B, F, G, I, and K the main topic for study was the question of regional planning, or political regionalization. The 1969 Minnesota Legislature had passed a Regional Planning Act, which laid the groundwork for regional development areas without specifying precisely how they would be structured politically or economically. A year later the governor delineated the boundaries of 11 such regions, leaving the formation of regional development commissions to the regions themselves.

Although the state law had been passed with little public attention or adverse publicity, leadership groups in community B had strongly questioned it. The editorials and feature articles of a daily newspaper in that community sharply challenged the procedure by which the law was enacted, the information the legislature used to prepare the law, and provisions of the law. That newspaper published in early 1970 a special report, written by two consulting economists, that was highly critical of the Regional Development Act. The editorial position of this newspaper, and its special report, was publicized in statewide media during the two months immediately preceding the survey. Each of the four communities in this group was a potential "regional center" economically and/or politically. Debate tended to center around the provisions of the act, the regional boundaries, and the question of which communities (if any) might be designated as regional growth centers. There were also debates over interpretation. At least one major newspaper in the state carried a feature article insisting that the regional center idea was not part of the act at all.

Interviews in communities A, B, G, and I were conducted in the fall of 1970. Two other communities in which regional planning was an issue, communities F and K, were studied in 1974. In these two communities, the regional planning issue was quite different. Communities F and K are in an 11-county region which was establishing a Regional Development Commission in another city, although location of the commission office was not itself a major point of contention. However, when the commission was being formed, there was a subregion organization representing five of the region's counties seeking state and federal funds for various projects in a way which seemed to compete with the larger organization. This situation had the potential for sharp regional conflict but it never materialized. In the summer of 1974, the subregion organization, beset by funding and administrative problems, became a technical agency subordinate to the larger commission. The conflict was defused and received little publicity; regional planning in these two communities, then, received only a small amount of media attention. Compared with communities A, B, G, and I, then, the regional planning topic in communities F and K was a low-intensity matter.

Community Group 4: Water Quality Issue

This community group included E, M, Q, and R, with interviewing conducted in the late winter and early spring of 1971. The issues in this study centered around either problems of local sewage control or mercury contamination of water. In this group of communities, each local issue was unique to the area.

In community E, the issue involved sewage control and two local levels of government, the city of E itself and the board of commissioners of the county in which community E is located. Prior to the study, a bill authorizing the county board to establish sewer or sewer-water districts in unincorporated areas, through local petition, had been introduced in the state legislature. Local debate on this procedure included the question of the impact on municipalities if establishment of such districts led to elimination of the need for annexation. While open debate with the state legislature and state agencies did not occur in this study, there was considerable intensity surrounding the question of control and financial responsibility. A position frequently taken by community councilmen was that if the city extended its sewer and water system to outlying areas, it should be accompanied by annexation of those areas in the interest of controlled urban growth. Representatives of outlying areas frequently opposed such annexation and ultimate political control by community E.

Community Q is a village with a longstanding sewage disposal problem. The village had been under state agency pressure to build a local sewage treatment system, and cost had been a major factor in the controversy. At one point, following editorial commentary by the local weekly newspaper on the situation (itself an unusual event in such situations), village council members had resigned. These events occurred within a few months preceding the survey. Shortly before interviewing began, the same local weekly announced that the sewage plan had put the village in the red.

The third community with a water quality issue was community R, located in an area in which agriculture and recreation are major sources of employment and income. More than a fourth of the labor force of the county is employed in agriculture. The community is on the shoreline of a large, popular recreational lake. In the late fall of 1970, the lake was named in a state-federal report about mercury levels in fish taken from a few selected bodies of water in the state. In the initial report, state health authorities had recommended that fish from this lake should be eaten only in limited quantities. The lake had been put on a mercury danger list along with a few other bodies of water in the state. This report received heavy publicity in statewide media and in the local weekly newspaper, which suggested editorially that the community had been treated arbitrarily and unfairly in the report and stood to lose its reputation as a popular resort. Consequently, the editorial said, the town was in danger of losing part of its seasonal business. After about half of the interviews had been completed, a new announcement from a state health agency indicated the lake was being taken off the mercury danger list of lakes. The new report had the effect of refuting the conclusions of the earlier one.

Community M was a striking example of a community suddenly faced with an unusual pollution problem and a crisis in local government. Community M is a residential and service community of about 25,000 when studied in 1971, reflecting a population growth of more than 500% since 1950. The community borders a river which is the source of drinking water for the central city downstream. During the spring thaw of 1971, unusually large amounts of water from melting snow led to a backup in sewer lines in community M, creating the possibility that sewage might back into basements of homes.

After checking with health officials from the city downstream, the city engineer in community M decided to treat some raw sewage with chlorine and release it into the river, upstream from where a major metropolitan area draws drinking water. This action immediately received extensive coverage in both newspapers and television stations covering the entire metropolitan area in which community M is located. The television stations and metropolitan newspapers emphasized the questions being raised by a state pollution control agency; one daily newspaper headline announced that community M might be "Sued over Sewage." The most widely circulating weekly newspaper in community M, however, emphasized local unity on the issue, so did another chain-owned weekly which prints a separate edition for community M. One weekly newspaper headline stated "City Council Commends Sewage Dumping Decision"; the other featured a headline "Mayor: Decision on Sewage Sound." Both weekly papers reported a city council resolution of commendation for the engineer's decision and expressed concern about how the metropolitan media, especially television, had covered the issue.

Community Group 5: The Power Line Issue

Communities O and S, the first in a predominantly agricultural area and the second in a metropolitan suburban and fringe area, are in the path of a corridor established for a high-voltage power line crossing the state of Minnesota. The power line was being sought by two electric power cooperatives which had tried earlier, without success, to negotiate easements with landowners along the proposed route. In early 1975, the cooperatives applied to a state agency for establishment of a 20-mile-wide corridor across the state, where a line route would be established. Under provisions of a recently enacted state law, this application led to a series of hearings in more than eight different communities, and eventually led to an agency decision to establish the corridor in much the same area as the utilities had requested. The hearings were adversary in character, with both the opposition groups and the utilities represented by legal counsel. The hearings were sequential, so that residents of one community might be told that their points were inappropriate at their hearing since the same topics had been covered previously in another community.

Of all the issues studied, the power line topic was most clearly characterized by organized hostility toward the external forces, in this case the utilities and the state agencies. One meeting was picketed by a group of local persons carrying signs, some of which characterized the power line project as a boon for big-city dwellers at farmers' expense. The opposition groups repeatedly contended that the lines would be dangerous to human and animal health, a nuisance to farming, injurious to the environment generally, and that local groups were not having an effective voice in the decision-making process.

Also, the power line received more concentrated attention from community weekly papers and for a longer period of time than any other topic studied. Weekly papers along the route, in both rural and suburban areas, highlighted opposition to the line, carried several letters to the editor opposing it (and a few favoring it), and devoted extensive space to discussion of the technical aspects of the issue. One resolution offered by farm groups was underground installation; this was rejected by the utility cooperatives as not feasible technically or economically. The interviews were conducted in both communities shortly before the state agency designated a power-line corridor which included both communities.

SUMMARY

In these 19 communities, data were gathered relating to the basic questions of the research project. These questions include the implications of community structure for media use and information environment, the role of newspapers in community controversy, the role of conflict in generating information and affecting the size of knowledge gaps, and the link between knowledge and opinions in different kinds of conflict situations.

These communities were selected because the community issues provided vehicles for the study of systems of information control, including generation, dissemination, and feedback processes. The study concentrates primarily on newspapers, although some evidence on broadcast media was gathered in a few of the communities. These data provide the basis for the analysis in the remainder of the book.

REFERENCES

BERELSON, B. and G. STEINER (1964) Human Behavior: An Inventory of Scientific Findings. New York: Harcourt Brace Jovanovich.

BETHELL, T. (1977) "The myth of an adversary press." Harpers Magazine (January): 33-40.

BRODER, D. S. (1977) "William T. Evjue memorial lecture." Presented at the meeting of the Association for Education in Journalism, Madison, Wisconsin, August.

COLEMAN, J. S. (1957) Community Conflict. New York: Macmillan.

COSER, L. A. (1967) Continuities in the Study of Social Conflict. New York: Macmillan.

――― (1956) The Functions of Social Conflict. New York: Macmillan.

DAHRENDORF, R. (1959) Class and Class Conflict in Industrial Society. Palo Alto, CA: Stanford University Press.

DONOHUE, G. A., P. J. TICHENOR, and C. N. OLIEN (1975) "Mass media and the knowledge gap: a hypothesis reconsidered." Communication Research 2: 3-23.

FESTINGER, L. (1957) A Theory of Cognitive Dissonance. Palo Alto, CA: Stanford University Press.

GERALD, E. J. (1963) The Social Responsibility of the Press. Minneapolis: University of Minnesota Press.

HENNESSY, B. (1975) Public Opinion. Belmont, CA: Wadsworth.

HULTENG, J. (1976) The Messenger's Motives: Ethical Problems of the News Media. Englewood Cliffs, NJ: Prentice-Hall.

HYMAN, H. and P. SHEATSLEY (1947) "Some reasons why information campaigns fail." Public Opinion Quarterly 11: 413-423.

KATZMAN, N. (1973) "The impact of communication technology: some theoretical premises and their implications." NIH Information Science Training Program Colloquium. Palo Alto, CA: Stanford University Press.

MARCEAU, F. J. (1972) "Communication and development: a reconsideration." Public Opinion Quarterly 26: 235-245.

OLIEN, C. N., G. A. DONOHUE, and P. J. TICHENOR (1978) "Community structure and media use." Journalism Quarterly 55: 445-455.

———— (1968) "The community editor's power and the reporting of conflict." Journalism Quarterly 45: 243-252.

PRIMACK, J. and F. VON HIPPEL (1974) Advice and Dissent: Scientists in the Political Arena. New York: Basic Books.

RIVERS, W. and W. SCHRAMM (1969) Responsibility in Mass Communication. New York: Harper & Row.

ROGERS, E. M. (1974) "Social structure and communication strategies in rural development: the communications effect gap and the second dimension of development." Presented at Cornell-CIAT International Symposium on Communication Strategies for Rural Development, Cali, Colombia.

SIGAL, L. V. (1973) Reporters and Officials: The Organization and Politics of Newsmaking. Lexington, MA: D. C. Heath.

SIMMEL, G. (1955) Conflict: The Web of Group Affiliation. New York: Macmillan.

SMALL, W. (1970) To Kill a Messenger: Television News and the Real World. New York: Hastings House.

STAR, S. and H. HUGHES (1950) "Report of an educational campaign: the Cincinnati Plan for the United Nations." American Journal of Sociology 55: 389-400.

TICHENOR, P. J., G. A. DONOHUE, and C. N. OLIEN (1970) "Mass media and differential growth in knowledge." Public Opinion Quarterly 34: 158-170.

WESTLEY, B. H. and M. MacLEAN (1957) "A conceptual model for communication research." Journalism Quarterly 34: 31-38.

WESTLEY, B. H. and W. SEVERIN (1963) "How Wisconsinites use and appraise their daily newspapers and other media." University of Wisconsin–Madison. (mimeo)

2

Methodology
in
Community Analysis

The basic unit of analysis in this research is the community. The focal questions and hypotheses relate to structural variation across communities. Data relating to citizen behavior and response are treated in several cases as community level measures, and sampling and measurement of citizens in each of the 19 communities are based largely on conventional survey research procedures. The nature of the questions and the analysis of the data from respondents are based on the development of hypotheses from a macrostructural perspective.

The primary independent variable of this research, community structure, is derived from data about organizational units of the community. Sample data, based on responses of individuals, are used to develop community level measures concerning conflict intensity, which is viewed as both a dependent variable and an independent variable in this analysis. The principal dependent variables are knowledge of issues and opinions about them.

SELECTION CRITERIA

The procedure adopted is based on selection of communities as conflict issues had developed, or as they appeared to be developing. In each community, a general population survey, an analysis of the type of structure which the community represented, and an analysis of newspaper content about the issue or issues under study were conducted.

Since a major variable under consideration was the acquisition of knowledge about community issues from mass media, it was essential to select topics that were receiving, or likely to receive, media attention. Topics were selected according to several specific criteria.

One, each issue had direct implications for the future of at least one community under study at a given time. In several situations, communities were selected so that a particular topic (such as mining or regional development) might be more salient at the particular time for one of those communities than for others. Degree of such salience varied and was treated as one of the independent variables for analysis.

Two, each issue had already received at least minimal media attention in at least one of the communities in a given study group. Considerable variation in media attention to issues existed across both topics and communities. Some issues had received high coverage in local papers and little or none in the statewide or metropolitan media; some had been covered in local and metropolitan media as well. In a few cases the heaviest publicity had been in metropolitan media, with less coverage in some of the local media. In every case, however, the media in at least one community in a grouping had given the topic major publicity.

Although coverage of issues was minimal in some cases, coverage of each issue involved more than printing a press release or using a single wire service story. Direct involvement of a local reporter or editor had occurred in at least one of the stories about the topic by the time of the survey. The index of mass media coverage of the issues was restricted to newspaper content. Radio and television coverage was not monitored.

Three, each issue involved the local community reacting to agencies or forces external to the community. In several communities some organized local activity occurred regarding the issue, but the issues would not have developed without some external force or initiating activity. The regional development issue stemmed largely from statewide legislation and from regional organizational activity coordinated and controlled to a considerable degree by a state planning agency. All of the issues in the metal industry grouping (mining, taconite, steel plant) involved the intervention or potential intervention by state and/or federal pollution control agencies. The power-line issue involved large utility associations, state agencies, and a state law that provided for one set of hearings for establishing a corridor and another for certifying the need for the power lines.

Variation existed in the extent to which local versus external organization was instrumental in creating the issue. Considerable local action took place in community E, where there was a question of establishing a sewage control district. In this case, the rural groups in the county were seeking an extension of the city's sewage district without annexation of the rural areas by the city. The proposal was constrained by the fact that state law did not permit the type of extension initially proposed and state enabling legislation was being considered. In community F, the city was providing sewage service for a suburb and there was a question about financing, as well as provision of service in compliance with state pollution control regulations.

At the other extreme, the *least* local organizational activity is illustrated by community R which, with virtually no forewarning, learned the state health department had determined that its popular recreational lake contained a high mercury level and was therefore polluted. The power-line topic was also near this extreme; the controversy developed when land was being sought by power utility associations for a high-voltage power line.

Four, each issue entailed public decisions which would be considered or made in an effort to resolve the question. While the locus of prospective decisions varied, the process for selection of communities and issues restricted the range of community conflicts studied. No cases were included in the study, for example, of labor-management disputes, such as between teachers and school boards or between steel plant workers and plant management. As the issues progressed, however, two cases of local political controversy, as well as several cases with some local division of views did develop. Many of these issues have the potential for rekindling smoldering divisions and animosities, creating complex conflict situations and making resolution more difficult.

AN INDEX OF COMMUNITY PLURALISM

One of the principal independent variables of the research is the degree of structural pluralism, which is defined as the extent to which one community is characterized by a greater diversity of potential sources of social power than another community. As the particular issues developed, communities were selected by groupings, described in Chapter 1. In some groupings, one selection criterion was variation in size, a major factor contributing to pluralism. In the metal industry grouping, for example, the selection of communities included a city of 100,000, one with about 7,000, and two under 5,000.

The operational definition of community pluralism is a summary of the community's rank position on five characteristics: (1) population of the municipality; (2) number of businesses in the community; (3) number of voluntary groups; (4) number of churches; and (5) number of schools and educational centers. Except for population, these measures were taken from telephone book listings from the communities. Each community was given a rank position, from 1 to 19, on each characteristic. These five rank scores were summed to provide an overall ranking of community pluralism. The raw values for these characteristics, and the overall pluralism rank score, are contained in Table 2-1, which also presents sample sizes and years when the communities were studied.

SAMPLING AND INTERVIEWING

The principal respondent group in each community was a sample of adults 21 and over, interviewed in their homes. In

Table 2-1 Sample Size and Characteristics of 19 Communities

Community	Sample Size	Year of Study	Population*	Voluntary Groups	Churches	Schools	Businesses	Rank on Pluralism Index	Sample Area
Nuclear Power Issue									
D	137	1969	39,700	47	40	34	1,848	17	city only
N	150	1969	2,900	5	15	8	265	8	surburban
P	148	1969	17,832	18	42	20	901	6.5	rural area
Mining and Metals Industries Issue									
C	134	1974	100,500	174	146	76	3,311	19	city only
H	117	1972	7,200	11	20	12	497	13	city only
L	101	1974	4,900	5	6	4	225	6.5	city only
J	91	1974	3,500	4	5	3	60	2	city only
Political Regionalization Issue									
A	99	1970	17,630	8	18	19	383	12	city & rural
B	88	1970	9,800	13	20	11	476	14	city & rural
I	92	1974	26,500	30	36	24	1,089	16	city only
G	99	1970	8,600	9	16	8	417	11	city & rural
I	93	1970	9,900	7	11	7	465	10	city & rural
K	183	1974	3,158	5	7	3	108	4	city & rural
Water Quality Issue									
I	94	1971	53,800	44	67	46	2,793	18	city & rural
M	125	1971	26,230	24	24	18	413	15	suburban
O	102	1971	600	1	4	1	48	1	city & rural
R	130	1971	2,500	4	7	3	176	3	city only
Power Line Issue									
O	136	1976	7,500	11	19	10	416	5	city & rural
S	140	1976	8,900	5	15	8	265	9	suburban

*Population refers to incorporated limits of the city or municipality within the sample area. The one exception is P, in which the sample was drawn from a rural area surrounding and near four communities, each with populations of 1,600 or less. The population figure for P is for the entire area sampled.

several cases, the definition of the community was the corporate limits of a town or city. In others, the sample areas included rural townships adjacent to the principal town or city. The sample designation depended upon the area for which the issue was relevant.

Sampling was conducted on an area probability basis, with the sample for each community area apportioned to different sections of town, city, or rural areas according to concentration of population. Within these sections—tracts, neighborhood zones, or townships—block or route designations were chosen at random, and interviewers were given specific instructions for selection of homes on those blocks or routes. Interviewers made initial respondent contacts at residences. Sex of respondent was partially controlled on a quota basis. The control was not entirely successful, however, since in several cases there were majorities (usually under 60%) of female respondents. This outcome resulted from a procedure that left it up to interviewers to get a balance of male and female respondents, rather than a specification for each individual interview. In communities where a perfect 50-50 split was not reached, the imbalance resulted primarily from sections of communities where the nature of the population (such as a retirement area with a disproportionate number of females) or work schedules made it extremely difficult for interviewers to adhere to the quota control.

INTERVIEWER CHARACTERISTICS AND COMPLETION RATES

The majority of the interviewers were local persons, contacted through county extension offices, who were recruited and trained for the specific interviewing task. Interviewers were frequently persons who had been active in organized adult and youth extension programs in the community and, therefore, had considerable experience in meeting and dealing with people generally. A small portion of the interviewing, under 10%, was conducted by members of the central project staff.

Local interviewing in each case was supervised by a project staff member. In a few cases, an experienced local interviewer served as a coordinator in the final phases of the surveying. Training sessions were conducted before interviewing by the project staff in each community. These sessions usually included between four and eight interviewers.

Interviewing procedures adopted for all 19 communities provided for replacement of only those residences which were vacant or where nobody was home after three house calls. Refusals were recorded for later contact, but not replaced. This procedure allowed for a detailed recording of initial refusal rates by area and interviewer, so that a different interviewer could contact residences where refusals had occurred and attempt to gain cooperation. The initial refusal rate for all interviewers was slightly over 9%. As a result of the follow-up procedure, however, the final completion rate average 91.7%.

Complete records of interviewer age, education, and prior interviewing experience were kept for 18 of the communities.[1] These records make possible an analysis of refusal rates according to the other three variables for 101 different interviewers. All except one of these interviewers were females, and 24 had prior interviewing experience before this project. Most of the prior experience was with commercial opinion polling forms; in two cases, the prior experience involved census enumeration.

Analysis of the refusal rates indicates very little difference according to prior interviewing experience. As indicated in Table 2-2, the overall refusal rate was 9.3% for those with prior interviewing experience and 9.2% for those who had done no survey interviewing before their first work with this project. A difference did exist in amount of interviewing done; those with prior experience averaged 35 completed interviews, and those without prior experience averaged 23. This difference appeared to be a result of the greater willingness of experienced interviewers to conduct additional interviews and to view the task as part of a continuing occupational pursuit. Persons without prior interviewing experience, on the other hand, typically took responsibility for 20 to 30 interviews apiece and, when those were completed, were either not available for further work or were not interested in doing more. Considerable variation appeared across individual communities. The highest refusal rate

Table 2-2 Initial Refusal Rates According to Prior
Interviewing Experience and Type of Interviewing
Location

	Interviewers *With* Prior Experience		Interviewers *Without* Prior Experience		Total	
Average initial refusal rate	9.3%	(24)*	9.2%	(77)	9.3%	(101)
Average number of interviews completed per interviewer**	35	(24)	23	(77)	26	(101)
Average initial refusal rate for:						
rural areas	4.9%	(3)	11.1%	(12)	9.9%	(15)
small towns	13.9%	(8)	9.1%	(20)	10.5%	(28)
small town & rural, combined	4.4%	(6)	6.4%	(20)	5.9%	(26)
cities	10.0%	(7)	10.7%	(25)	10.6%	(32)
Average initial refusal rate for interviewers who are:						
under 30	37.0%	(1)	15.2%	(15)	16.6%	(16)
31-40	11.5%	(5)	9.9%	(28)	10.2%	(33)
41-50	6.5%	(12)	5.8%	(23)	6.0%	(35)
over 50	8.3%	(6)	6.5%	(11)	7.1%	(17)

*Numbers in parentheses refer to number of interviewers upon which the refusal rate is based.
**Number of interviews completed and usable, not including refusals.

was in a small town and the lowest was in a rural area. Four communities had initial refusal rates of under 5% and six, over 12%.

Interviewer age appears to be a factor with the sharpest difference occurring between interviewers under 30 and over 30 years of age. The 16 interviewers under 30 had average refusal rates of 16%, highest of all. The rate is 10.2% for the 31-40 group, 6% for the 41-50 group, and 7.1% for those over 50.

Thus, age appears to be a more important variable than experience in predicting refusal rates. In addition to the possible effects of maturation and confidence, a strong possibility exists that the method of recruiting through extension agencies may have produced a cadre of senior persons whose ability to deal with a variety of interpersonal situations had been developed through a lifetime of community organizational and service work. A number of the persons who did interviewing clearly did it out of a sense of service to the university and/or the local extension program.   •

The analysis of interviewer performance according to age, experience, and area also raises a number of questions that cannot be answered. For example, were older interviewers, recruited through local agencies, more likely to know the respondents and to use personal friendship as a basis for gaining cooperation? A parallel possibility is that if the interviewers are known locally, i.e., their names are recognized or they are known personally by the respondent, this procedure imparts a sense of obligation not only to the interviewers but also to the respondents to complete the interview. The training and assigning procedures did take the question of personal friendship into account, and the policy was to assign interviewers to parts of town or rural areas where they were least likely to know the respondents. This procedure, however, would not necessarily cover situations in which the interviewer may be known as a leader by many respondents with whom the interviewer is not acquainted personally. Such situations might occur frequently with extension program leaders. The possible biases from this interviewing procedure are not known, but should be recognized as a possible limitation from interviewer selection procedures.

COMMUNITY LEADERS AND NEWS SOURCES

In addition to the general population samples, selected individuals were interviewed in the four communities in the mining and metal industry group, in two of the communities in the political regionalization group, and in both communities in the power-line group. The selected individuals were local leaders, specialists on the topic under study, reporters or editors of local newspapers, and, in one case, broadcast station reporters. These interviews served two main purposes: to provide additional background information on the issues under study and to measure similarities and differences in perceptions between leader and media groups and samples of the general public.

● OPERATIONAL MEASURES

The interview schedules varied according to the topic under study but contained several common items on media use and preference. In each community, the opening question was, "Between television, radio, and the newspapers, which *one* do you prefer most as a source of news these days?" This was followed by questions about specific newspapers read, frequency of reading, and time spent watching television.

Developing measures of knowledge that would be comparable across topics and communities presented a special methodological problem. The basic measure was an open-ended item:

Have you seen or heard anything about (issue under study)? If yes
Can you recall what you've seen or heard recently?

Two additional probes were used with this question. Persons who had conducted an analysis of the topic and of news articles coded the open-end responses according to the number of accurate and inaccurate statements which the respondents made.

While this open-end measure of knowledge and coding procedure produces distributions that may depart from normality, it has the advantage of comparability across topics as well as across communities. It was not the only knowledge measure used. In several communities, additional items were used to measure level of knowledge about specific aspects of the topic.

PERCEPTION OF CONFLICT

Respondent perception of conflict was measured in two ways. In the first three communities studied, the measure of perception of conflict was based upon a separate coding of the same responses given to the open-end knowledge item. A determination was made of whether the response included statements about differences in views, confrontations, divisions, or tensions in the community. Each response was coded in a dichotomous fashion, according to whether there was an indication of conflict.

In the final 16 communities, a separate item designed to measure perception of intensity of conflict was included. The question was, "Would you say that [issue being studied] is a touchy subject around here or not?" The assumption is that the higher the percent saying yes, the more intense the conflict is in the community as a whole. The touchy subject question tended to produce a higher proportion of respondents giving the conflict answer. There was some correspondence between the two measures; in eight communities where the open-end responses were coded for conflict and where the touchy subject question was also used, the rank correlation between the two measures was .65 (p = .05).

MEASURES OF ATTITUDES AND OPINIONS

Measures of community attitudes and opinions toward the various issues were based upon at least four-item question scales. These scales are specific to the individual issues and topics and are comparable across communities only where identical items are asked. The response categories were "agree" or "disagree" for all attitude and opinion items, and the scales were self-administered.

INTERPERSONAL COMMUNICATION

In most cases, respondents were asked, "Have you talked with other people recently about the [issue under study]?" The proportion answering yes was taken as a measure of the level of interpersonal communication about the issue for that community.

SUMMARY

Data for the analysis of the 19 communities are based upon evidence gathered from existing documents, from newspaper articles, from interviews with samples of adult respondents in the communities, and, in some cases, from interviews with individuals in media and community leadership positions. A community pluralism index was constructed as an indicator of the principal independent variable in the study. Conflict intensity and community knowledge levels are based upon aggregated data from the sample of interviewees in each community. Interviewing was done mostly by hired interviewers who, in many cases, were local residents hired and trained for the particular project.

The question often arises within the discipline about the aggregation of individual responses and their utilization for purposes of structural analysis. The structural theory, of course, calls for the determination of individual behavior within the context of the structure and also attributes those behaviors to the nature of the structural variable under consideration. It is not simply a matter of the response of the individual but rather the nature of the hypothesis and the subsequent structuring of questions related to the theoretical hypotheses under inquiry that become the salient questions with respect to unit of analysis and interpretation. Thus, the macroscopic structural approach or 'holistic' frame of reference does involve the inquiry into individual behavior and at times the aggregation of their responses. But both the nature of the inquiry and the treatment of the aggregated responses provide the fundamental basis of interpretation and testing of hypotheses.

NOTE

1. In one of the community studies, interviewing was done partly by students in a graduate seminar and partly by hired interviewers. In that case, data on performance of the hired interviewers were inadvertently destroyed before the analysis of the entire 19 communities was completed.

3

Newspaper Type
and
Citizen Media Use

Newspapers are basically creations of the communities they serve. Their size, nature, scope, and content are to a large extent determined by the characteristics of the surrounding town or city and the region in which that town or city exists. One readily available body of evidence testifying to the relationship between community size, newspaper type, and circulation is the newspaper directory of nearly any state. In Minnesota, there are 293 communities with populations of 10,000 or less. All except four of them have newspapers which are published once or twice a week. For the 42 places with populations above that level, 23 have dailies (Minnesota Newspaper Association, 1976). In an Iowa study, the correlation between community population and newspaper circulation was .84 (Whiting, 1976).

To argue that media are shaped by their communities may seem to slight the differences in journalistic skill and publishing entrepreneurship that may occur from one community to another. Differences may indeed exist, but the possible range of their effects is apparently quite constricted because of basic community characteristics that may limit circulation, advertising support, and, therefore, newspaper income. Stone (1975), for example, compared a sample of weekly newspapers with a sample of small daily newspapers in an analysis of business volume and profit. Even though his daily newspapers had circulations of 25,000 or under (because of the particular population of dailies he was studying), they nevertheless had annual net profits that averaged about three times those of weeklies, which had much smaller circulations as a result of being published in smaller communities. Income potential appears to be a fundamental criterion for deciding whether a publisher will operate a weekly or a daily, and the choice will have several consequences for how the newspaper will serve the community. "Going daily," as publishers often put it, means more total space, more state and national news, and more frequent advertising as well as more advertising in total.

Community pluralism, a basic structural variable in the study of the 19 communities, affects media structure, citizen use of media, and decision-making processes within society (DeFleur and Ball-Rokeach, 1975).

Population size is a readily measured characteristic of community structure. Other quantitative indicators of pluralism (number of businesses, churches, schools, and voluntary groups as described in Chapter 1) are closely related to community population size. The rank correlation between the combined pluralism index and population size across the 19 communities is .75.

One of the most frequently stated generalizations in the social sciences is that patterns of behavior vary according to social structure. In the community setting, different patterns of behavior may be observed in both individual and collective modes of making public decisions. Communities low on the pluralism dimension, as typified by the isolated rural town, ordinarily make public decisions in ways based on tradition and conducted in an atmosphere of general consensus. Such a pattern of decision making is likely to occur in any social structure having relatively low degrees of differentiation in occupation, organization, cultural and religious interests, leisure time pursuits, and professional services.

The "interlocking directorate" is a characteristic of systems in which there is a homogenization of power. Where there is a low degree of differentiation in social organization, individuals who are socially powerful in one sector tend to be powerful in others. A leading businessman may very well be a member of the city council, the school board, and the church board of trustees. Such an organizational state may lead to a great deal of personal satisfaction and a high self perception among high-status persons of their personal ability to affect public affairs in the small community (Finifter and Abramson, 1975).

Where relative homogeneity leads to the interlocking direc-torate, the predictable tendency is to conduct public affairs in all institutions at the managerial level with a minimum of public exposure of controversial matters. Public decision making gen-erally operates on a relatively interpersonal basis among a power elite, and, as data from several studies indicate, norms relating to distribution of information tend to support this pattern among both media and leadership groups. Evidence from an earlier study of 88 Minnesota communities (Olien, Donohue, and Tichenor, 1968) indicated that newspapers are more likely to avoid reporting internal conflict in the small, more tradi-tional community in the interest of maintaining an outward image of tranquillity as well as tranquillity in fact.

The more highly educated segment of a small community has a relatively high opportunity to dominate leadership positions. However, the leadership skill required in such a traditionally oriented community may lead to a trained incapacity to operate effectively in negotiations between the more diverse and plural-istic state, regional, and national structures on the one hand and the local structures on the other. Any given individual leader may be able to develop both the skills necessary for functioning in the more intimate environment of the local community and those for a more secondary system with which the local com-munity has interdependencies. However, developing these skills requires a role differentiation on the part of leadership that may be rather complex and unappreciated by local citizens. For example, behavior of state and national political leaders may appear quite inconsistent when citizens compare their capital city statements with statements the same leaders make when they visit the hometown or the local region.

A similar problem in role differentiation may be seen in financial agencies and in newspapers. The independent banker in a rural community is in a position similar to that of local political leaders. This banker must deal in everyday matters with tradition-oriented clientele and, at the same time, must relate to banking agencies of the larger society. In like manner, the small-town editor is addressing local traditions while recognizing that maintenance of those traditions is highly dependent upon what happens in society as a whole. Like other leaders, editors must deal in both systems and, therefore, may appear inconsistent at times. An editor might be active in a statewide organization of journalists dedicated to increasing access of reporters to information from public agencies, yet justify editorially a local school board's defiance of an open-meeting law as essential for local harmony.

In the urban community, the social structure is much more differentiated (Mott, 1973). The more pluralistic structure of the urban center produces quite different needs for communication compared with the small, more homogeneous community (Meier, 1962). As communities increase in size, they become more diversified horizontally and vertically (Wilson, 1973). Increasing size often brings a multiplicity of functions and numerous centers of social power. While size and structural pluralism are conceptually separate, they are interrelated in such a way that one may lead to the other. Growth often produces differentiation on many dimensions, including more segmentation of institutions and more compartmentalization of functions (Campbell, 1970). The greater diversity in sources of employment, interest groups, professional groups, educational and religious organizations, political associations, and public agencies increases the sources of actual or potential power and influence. These power centers are interdependent and are also far more specialized than would be true in a smaller community.

There is a rather widespread assumption that size leads to mass society and standardization, but this assumption may be quite misleading. As indicated above, as the population increases, differentiation tends to increase. In this process, the standardization that does occur takes place within each of the differentiated groups, so that the result is segmental standardization but not general uniformity. The outcome then is not homogenization in the community as a whole, but rather increased degrees of heterogeneity.

Size has another effect on pluralism which to some extent goes beyond the existence of sheer differences in function and interest. That effect is the result of critical size for social organization and influence. An occupational group that comprises 5% of a town of 1,000 workers has such a small base for organization that effectiveness in representing its 50 members is unlikely if not impossible. On the other hand, 5% of a labor force of 100,000 or more workers produces a sufficient critical mass for effective organization. A group can be, say, an ethnic minority and still have the necessary numbers to organize and "make itself heard" in a larger community.

Decision making in the larger community necessarily must take pluralism into account. The process is forced to consider the differing and often conflicting interests of the various groups. In dealing with these diverse interests, pluralistic communities have a greater need for generation and use of formalized knowledge. The more complex the community, the greater the need for knowledge of other parts by any one segment. A neighborhood group or a union local continually faces a need to "know what's going on" in business, in government, and in related interest groups. These needs are accompanied by the fact that specialization itself requires a need for knowledge. Across large-scale social structures, for example, occupational differentiation and level of education are strongly correlated (Blau, 1975).

The greater reliance on formal dissemination of knowledge in more heterogeneous social systems has been noted frequently (Benson, 1973). Such a community requires coordination and, compared with more homogeneous communities, has more mechanisms for ameliorating conflict as well as for facilitating greater communication among its parts (Morris and Rein, 1973). One of these mechanisms is the daily newspaper, which may be relied upon to communicate different views and to enter the social action process at an earlier stage. Whereas small community leaders may strive to initiate and legitimize new ideas before they get into the local newspaper, groups in the larger community may rely directly upon the mass media for reaching potential legitimizers. A new idea may be reported in the press of the larger community as a "trial balloon" to test public reaction. Conflicts in the city council and county board meeting may, in some instances, be transmitted to much of the community leadership through the newspaper. Thus, reporting governmental conflict in the daily newspapers of larger and more pluralistic communities may have the dual functions of legitimizing social action *and* maintaining political discourse.

The more frequent attention to conflict in the newspapers of larger metropolitan areas does not necessarily mean reporting "conflict for conflict's sake"; the metropolitan papers are also likely to be closely attuned to questions of compromise in negotiations and disputes. The nature of a pluralistic society reduces the probability that any one group will dominate, in general, since there are so many sources of organizational power, and it also increases the probability that any one group will have to compromise with others in resolving a given problem. Hence, there is the necessity of compromising among the leadership if conflict among special interest groups is not to lead to a stalemate with possible negative consequences for the system as a whole. Recent prolonged strikes between airlines and pilots and between workers and management in mining and other industries are examples. In such controversies, the compromise perspective is a view of continuous adjustment rather than a series of individual crises.

COMMUNITY STRUCTURE AND ATTENTION TO MEDIA

If newspapers and other media are shaped by their communities, then one would expect that citizen use of these media would also differ according to community characteristics. In terms of maintaining a well-informed public, this is an important question. Findings from several studies, for example, support the conclusion that the higher the use of and preference for print media, the higher the level of information about public affairs topics (Robinson, 1967; Schramm and Wade, 1967; Clarke and Fredin, 1978).

Theoretically, daily newspaper reading is expected to be higher and television use lower in communities in which the principal local newspaper is a daily rather than a weekly. Correspondingly, preferences for newspapers as a source of news is expected to be lower, and preference for television higher, in weekly newspaper communities than in larger and more pluralistic communities served by daily papers. Communities with twice-weekly papers would be expected to be intermediate on these measures. The emphasis is on television rather than radio, since television is the major broadcast source of news among citizens nationally (An Extended View of Public Attitudes Toward Television and Other Mass Media, 1977).

Since weekly newspapers are most likely to exist in smaller and relatively homogeneous communities, they concentrate on news about existing institutions and on the consensus aspect of local affairs. Considerable evidence suggests that part of the function of weekly papers is to maintain a state of tranquillity, thus avoiding social disruption of small community relationships. Within these relationships, which are based upon personal contact and communication patterns, disruptions are not tolerated efficiently (Donohue, Tichenor, and Olien, 1973; Edelstein and Schulz, 1963; Janowitz, 1952). Concentration on local topics tends to dominate the weekly to the exclusion of external matters. Therefore, since most conflicts in these communities involve interdependencies with external agencies, a newspaper tends to exclude conflict to the extent that it excludes reports about external groups. This also means that when the local newspaper *does* report conflict, it concentrates primarily on conflicts involving external groups.

If a community is more pluralistic, it is more likely to be served by a daily newspaper, which tends to report a broader range of local as well as state and national news. Because of the pressures from competing sources that occur in a pluralistic structure, the daily newspaper is more likely to emphasize the controversial aspect of public issues. This reporting has the function of maintaining communication among the multiple interest groups in the community and in society at large.

Characteristics of the medium reporting events and issues of that community would be likely to play some role in determining the absolute and relative attention that citizens pay to media as a whole. Weekly newspapers may be highly valued for their reflection of the local scene, but they occupy only a small portion of the citizenry's time and attention in the process. Their emphasis on social consensus, however satisfying it may be, is not necessarily a strong stimulus for reading. Therefore, when television is universally available, one might expect it to be used heavily for a variety of reasons. With its combined audio and visual dramatization, it appeals to broad audience segments and, like the local weekly, to the dominant values in society (Gerbner and Gross, 1976). Television programming however, not being local but national in scope, is structured to be especially cognizant of the conflict issues in the larger society. Although Gerbner and Gross contend that attention to *violent* conflict in entertainment programming stems from the economy dramatization that violence provides, it is also quite possible that the systematic selection of intense conflicts in news and documentary programming results from more than a choice of dramatic symbols. Television may well be structured so as to be especially cognizant of the needs of various power groups in the social system, as is the local weekly, and, consequently, of the conflicts that threaten the values that both media generally reinforce. Newspapers, while identifying conflict in a similar way, generally are more attuned to a specific community, whereas television viewing may not be linked to community identity to the same degree. The small community context of the weekly places it in a position of conflict suppression, in contrast to television news programming which occurs across communities.

Strong community ties are major forces leading to reading the local newspaper. Therefore, if a community is served by a weekly newspaper, a regional daily paper does not have the same local meaning regardless of how easy it is to receive. In spite of its regional coverage, a daily paper from a more or less distant and larger city does not address local concerns the way the hometown weekly does, or the way the daily itself does for its own urban locality. Regional dailies do not cover the local routine in outlying towns, but highlight only the more unusual occurrences in those places. When small town residents read about their community in the regional daily, they are seeing their town through the lenses of a distant city rather than through the eyes of neighbors and local institutions. Theoretically, then, newspapers depend upon their link to community identity in fulfilling their functions (Bogart and Orenstein, 1965). If none of the available daily papers serves that link, citizens may be less likely to have the same attachment for newspapers as a whole, even if they *are* attached to local weekly papers.

It might be countered that the regional daily newspaper reflects economic unity of a region, through advertising as well as through business news. However, the idea that economic integration leads to *political* integration and therefore identity may not be correct, even though proposals for establishing national or regional policies on matters such as energy production and control may be based on such an assumption. Accepting the idea of economic interdependency of a region does not necessarily mean identifying with that region in the same sense as identifying with a community. Community loyalties may in principle not be transferrable to larger political units. Identity with regions may be fundamentally different from that of communities. That is, nation, state, county, and community are all part of a citizen's identity, but they have quite different connotations for behavior.

The reasoning thus far applies to larger cities and smaller separated towns. But what about suburban areas served by weeklies? Would the easy availability of metropolitan dailies lead to high dependence on newspapers as in the urban center itself? According to the perspective here, the expected answer would be no, acknowledging the likelihood that suburbanite reading of the big city daily varies directly with the strength of the suburbanites' ties to that city (Bogart and Orenstein, 1965). Most individual suburbs are relatively homogeneous segments of diverse metropolitan areas. As bedroom communities they tend to have a relatively narrow range of residents in terms of socioeconomic status and ethnic background. In such a setting, a weekly newspaper may fulfill the same functions as a weekly in a small rural town, so that middle-class suburbanites would be relatively unattached to other newspapers. Just as reading about one's hometown in a regional daily is not the same as reading about it in the local weekly, reading about one's suburb in the "neighborhood" section of a metro daily may be far different from seeing it in the suburban community press. Also, the downtown conflict reported in the metro daily may be seen as irrelevant to the suburbanite who neither votes in nor strongly identifies with the inner city, however dependent he or she may be on that city for jobs, shopping, and recreation. A question might be raised as to whether the metropolitan daily might have a quite select audience for news purposes, a relatively sophisticated segment of the total population which views life in a more cosmopolitan way than is true for the average socioeconomic level in the population. Thus, the metro daily may be several papers in one—none of which may be very well done, hence its current plight.

If the foregoing analysis of social structure is reasonably valid, then citizen use of media and preferences among media for news should differ according to community structure and type of newspaper available. Several measures were employed in the 19 communities to test the hypotheses stated above. These hypotheses are, first, that daily newspaper reading is expected to be higher and television use lower in communities in which the principal local newspaper is a daily rather than a weekly. The second is that preference for newspapers as a source of news is expected to be lower, and preference for television higher, in weekly newspaper communities than in larger and more pluralistic communities served by daily papers.

Daily newspaper use in each of the 19 communities was measured as the average number of daily papers which respondents reported reading twice per week or more. Television use is average hours reported spent viewing each day. Preference measures for each medium are based upon answers to the following question "Between television, radio, and the newspapers, which *one* do you prefer most as a source of news these days?"[1] Since it is a forced-choice question, this item may tend to underestimate respondent evaluations of media in an absolute sense (Carter and Greenberg, 1964). However, since actual use is measured separately, this item was chosen for use across communities on the assumption that it provides a reliable indicator of community differences.

DAILY VERSUS WEEKLY NEWSPAPERS AND PLURALISM

Among the 19 communities studied, the smaller ones have weeklies and the larger ones had dailies. The 10 communities with weeklies average 5,770 in population, with an average of 288 businesses per community (Table 3-1). By contrast, the six communities with daily newspapers average nearly 40,000 in population, with 1,650 businesses each. The three semiweekly newspaper communities are intermediate on all pluralism measures, although they are clearly more like the weekly than the daily newspaper communities.

Community size and pluralism is also reflected in differences in newspaper content. In both weekly and semiweekly newspapers, about 90% of the news space is devoted to local news, with under 10% in state and national news and public affairs. By contrast, the dailies devote under half of their newshole (40%) to local news and public affairs, and well over half (56%) to state and national public affairs. However, proportion of total space devoted to local *public affairs* news differs little among weeklies, semiweeklies, and dailies. The bulk of the news in the papers in the smaller, less pluralistic communities is social

Table 3-1 Characteristics of Communities and Their Newspaper Content

Community Characteristics	Weekly Newspaper Towns (N:10)	Semi-Weekly Newspaper Towns (N:3)	Daily Newspaper Towns (N:6)
Average population	5,770.00	8,533.00	39,733.00
Average number of businesses	288	460	1,650
Average number of voluntary groups	8.20	9.00	52.67
Average number of churches	14.40	15.67	54.50
Average number of schools	7.80	9.00	35.00
Newspaper Content Characteristics*			
Newshole, average size in column inches per edition	1,058.00	959.00	1,349.00
Average percent newshole devoted to *all* local news and public affairs	90.80%	90.00%	40.50%
Average percent newshole devoted *to local public affairs only*	21.00%	19.33%	17.83%
Average percent of newshole devoted to *state and national public affairs*	7.3%	8.7%	55.8%

*Contents measures are based on per-edition averages for all editions published the month before the survey study was conducted.
Table reprinted by permission of *Journalism Quarterly*

events and athletics, quite apart from political news or reports of public agencies and institutions.

CITIZEN USE OF DAILY NEWSPAPERS AND TELEVISION

The structural frame of reference suggests that in smaller communities where the local paper published is a weekly rather than a daily, reading daily newspapers will be lower and viewing television will be higher. The data on newspaper reading and television viewing (Figures 3-1 and 3-2) tend to support both aspects of that hypothesis. In Figure 3-1, for example, average daily reading is higher in each of the six daily-newspaper communities than in any one of the nondaily communities. Corres-

Figure 3.1   Type of Newspaper and Mean Daily
Reading in 19 Communities

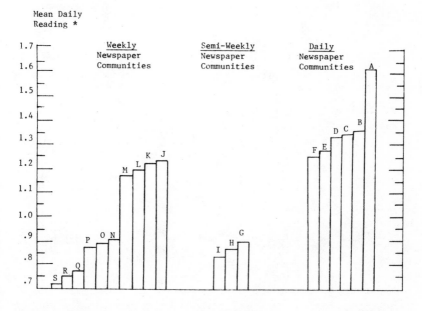

* "Mean Daily Reading" refers to the average of daily newspapers reported as read twice per week or more by respondents in each community.

Difference between communities p < .025 by Mann-Whitney U Test, weeklies compared with others.

Reprinted by permission of *Journalism Quarterly*

pondingly, as indicated in Figure 3-2, television viewing tends to be higher in the communities served by weeklies than in communities served by dailies.

There are two specific findings in Figures 3-1 and 3-2, which may reflect a rather complex set of relationships between community structure and utilization of newspapers and television. One of these findings is that weekly communities S (lowest daily reading of all), M, and N are metropolitan suburbs, contiguous to each other, in a county in which morning and evening daily papers with circulations in excess of 200,000 each are published. The second is that in the three communities

Figure 3.2   Type of Newspaper and Median TV Viewing in 19 Communities

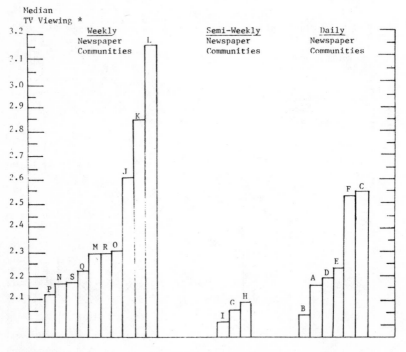

* "Mean Television Viewing" is the median number of hours of daily viewing reported by respondents in each community.

Difference between communities, p < .05 by Mann-Whitney U Test, weeklies against others.

Reprinted by permission of *Journalism Quarterly*

served by semiweekly papers, daily newspaper reading *and* television viewing are extremely low, which is not consistent with the expectation that communities with semiweeklies would be intermediate on all measures. All three are similar in size and are in predominantly rural areas that are well outside the fringes of urban centers where dailies are published.

The relationship between weekly newspaper availability and use of other media is also illustrated by a comparison of level of weekly reading with level of daily reading across the 19 communities. The rank correlation coefficient for weekly and daily reading is −.52, significant at the .05 level; for weekly reading and television viewing it is positive as expected (.35) but not significant at the .05 level.

In general, then, data support the hypotheses about media use generated from a structural perspective. A more pluralistic community has a media mix which differs in amount and kind from that of a more homogeneous community. The greater number of media alternatives available in the urban center tends to work against use of television at levels as high as in the small community where the options are more limited and where the functions of media are different. Also, reading a daily newspaper tends to be higher in the urban community where the newspaper is directed toward the concerns of that community and its linkages with the larger society. *Both* daily newspaper reading and television viewing tend to vary as predicted according to structural differences.

TYPE OF COMMUNITY AND CITIZEN MEDIA PREFERENCE FOR NEWS

Community analysis also tends to support the hypothesis that *preference* for newspapers as a source of news will be lower, and *preference* for television will be higher, in less pluralistic communities served by weekly newspaper communities than in more pluralistic communities served by daily papers.[2] Findings for percent of respondents mentioning newspapers as a "preferred source of news" are in Figure 3-3 for the

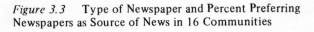

Figure 3.3   Type of Newspaper and Percent Preferring
Newspapers as Source of News in 16 Communities

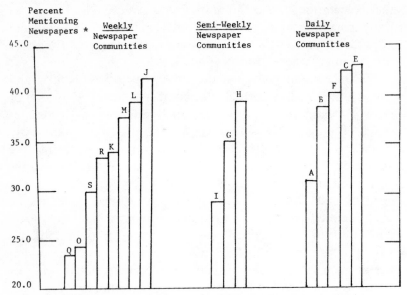

* The question asked in each community was "Between television, radio, and the
newspapers, which one do you prefer most as a source of news these days?" The
three first communities stuidied—Osseo, St. Cloud, and Wright County—are not
included, since the item was worded differently in those cases.

Reprinted by permission of *Journalism Quarterly*

16 communities where the question was asked. Four of the five
daily communities are at or near the top of the distribution.
The fifth, community A with under 35% mentioning newspapers, has one of the smallest dailies (in circulation) in the
Midwest. Weekly and semiweekly newspaper communities tend
to be lower on newspaper preference than daily newspaper
communities.

Similarly, preference for television as a source of news is
higher in the communities served by weeklies (Figure 3-4), with
daily communities lower. As with newspaper preference, semiweekly newspaper communities also tend to be intermediate on
television preference.

From the above two hypotheses linking community pluralism
to media preferences and to media use, it follows that level of
weekly reading should be negatively related to preference for

Figure 3.4   Type of Newspaper and Percent
Preferring TV as Source of News in 16 Communities

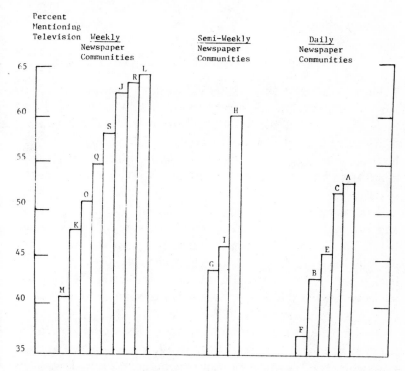

Difference between communities p < .05 by Mann-Whitney U Test, weeklies
against others.

Reprinted by permission of *Journalism Quarterly*

newspapers as a news source and positively related to television
preference. Both of these expectations are borne out by the
data. Across these 16 communities, the rank correlation between level of weekly reading and preference for newspapers is
-.52. The rank correlation between level of weekly reading and
television preference is .50, and the rank correlation between
level of daily reading and preference for newspapers is .59. All
of these correlations are significant at the .05 level. The rank
correlation between daily reading and preference for television
is -.36 (p > .05).

The above findings indicate a consistent pattern of support

for the hypotheses about the relationship between the independent variable of community structure and the dependent variables of media structure and media use and preference by citizens.

COMMUNITY LEVELS OF EDUCATION

There is a question whether education might be a key variable underlying the observed differences in media uses and preferences among communities. The more pluralistic communities served by dailies in the study also have higher average levels of education. But does education itself make a difference, apart from the fact that a community has a particular media structure?

The rank correlations between community level of education and use and preference measures are consistently weaker than between community pluralism ranking and media scores. For example, the rank correlation between pluralism and daily newspaper reading across the 19 communities is .64 (p < .01) whereas the correlation between *educational level* and *daily newspaper reading level* is .22 (> .20).

As a further check, communities are classified according to whether their median level of education is under or over 12 years (Figures 3-5 and 3-6). Among communities with weeklies or semiweeklies, little difference in reading appears, with both high and low education communities spread across the range. The only daily newspaper community with education below the median level is B, which is second highest on the daily reading score in Figure 3-1.

Community level of education may, however, be somewhat of a factor in newspaper *preference* when community type is controlled (Figure 3-6). Among high education communities with nondaily papers, three are next to the top of the distribution on newspaper preference, but two are well below the middle of the range for smaller papers. The one daily newspaper community with low education is second lowest of the five daily communities on the preference measure.

Figure 3.5 Mean Daily Newspaper Reading According to Type of Newspaper and Level of Education in 19 Minnesota Communities

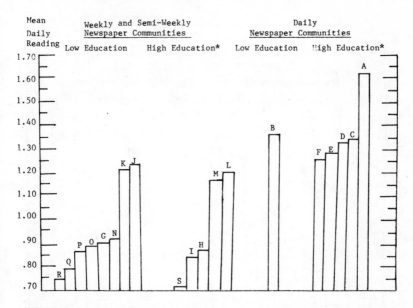

* High Education includes communities with a median level of education of 12 years or higher.

Reprinted by permission of *Journalism Quarterly*

In general, the principal differences are by type of community and type of medium, which go together. While level of education may be a related factor, it appears to be secondary to community structure. That is, when community level of media use is analyzed by controlling structure and allowing community level of education to vary, the sharpest differences are according to type of community structure.

It should be emphasized that the education analysis reported above is based on the differences *between* communities. *Within* each of the communities, educational level of individuals is associated with individual use and preferences in the following ways: The within-community correlations between education and daily newspaper reading are positive and significant

Figure 3.6   Percent Preferring Newspapers as a Source
of News, According to Type of Newspaper and Level
of Education in 16 Minnesota Communities

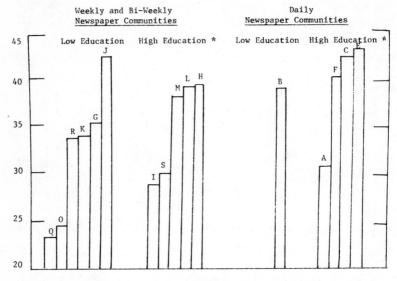

* "High Education" includes communities with a median level of education of
12 years or higher.

Reprinted by permission of *Journalism Quarterly*

($p < .05$) in 8 of the 19 communities; the correlations with
television viewing are negative and significant in 6 communities.
The correlations at the individual level between education and
preference for newspapers are significant in 4 communities.
These within-community correlations are generally consistent
with other findings based on individual level analysis of media
use and preference (Westley and Severin, 1963; Greenberg and
Dervin, 1967).

MEDIA USES AND PREFERENCES IN SUBURBAN AREAS

The central nature of the media structure is emphasized by
three communities which are suburban, rather than rural, and

are served by weekly papers. Citizens in suburban communities often have choices among media that may be different both qualitatively and quantitatively from choices in outlying towns or in central cities. Such a high level of choice among print media may not produce a high community-wide orientation toward newspapers but may instead lead to a higher degree of specialization in media use *within* such a community. Increasing specialization in media use would mean, in effect, that print media are competing for reader attention in those communities.

If weeklies and dailies are competing for attention in suburbs, the process would be quite different from that analyzed by Janowitz (1952), who saw the community newspaper in the Chicago suburban area in the immediate post-World War II decade as an *auxiliary* to the daily press. His interpretation appears to rest heavily on the point that the community press deals largely with local news and relatively little with state, national, or international topics. This gap in extralocal content, then, would be filled by the large daily newspapers from metropolitan centers.

Bogart and Orenstein's (1965) analysis follows similar reasoning. They concluded that the local weekly paper in "Intercity" had little bearing on the ability of the daily newspaper from a nearby larger city to find readers. They concluded that the high degree of detail in the weekly, in such areas as real estate listings and neighborhood news, serves to supplement rather than conflict with daily spot news coverage by dailies from outside.

Since Janowitz's study, however, television has become an important part of the American scene, especially for the highlights of international and national news. In this respect, television may compete with and replace the daily to some extent, so that the suburban weekly may in fact be more supplemental to television than to the daily newspaper.

Although the results should be viewed with caution, data from the three suburban communities (communities M, N, and S) do raise some questions about the "complementarity" hypothesis. Community S has the lowest daily reading in the entire group of 19 communities, even though its educational level is above the median. Neither community S nor the other two stands apart from the remaining seven communities served by weeklies on reading of daily papers. However, the three do tend to be low on television viewing. The essential point here is that, contrary to what one might expect from the Janowitz interpretation, the suburban communities are lower in daily newspaper reading than in cities where the paper being published is a daily.

All three of these suburban areas have undergone considerable change in recent decades. Community S is an older town which, since World War II, has been overtaken by suburban sprawl and now has a large component of residents commuting to the central city and another of older and retired citizens. Community M is relatively new, with large tracts of upper-middle-class homes and apartments. Community M has grown by more than 500% since 1950. Community N is a mixture of new residential areas and open country farms and residences.

Limited as these findings are to three suburban areas, low daily newspaper reading in such areas may underscore the fact that metropolitan newspapers often find it difficult to maintain circulation in their nearby suburbs. Although the data here do not fully address the point, one might speculate whether the "complementary reading" hypothesis will continue to apply as television becomes an increasingly important factor in providing national and international news and as media structural changes contribute to a changing total structure and to changing behavior within it. In his recent analysis, Bogart (1975) argues that the suburban *daily* (usually an evening paper) provides stronger competition for the larger newspaper from the central city. Nevertheless, the same reasoning may apply for a weekly newspaper *if* increasing amounts of television news coverage tend to draw attention away from newspaper reading generally. Television may have far greater ability to satisfy felt needs for national news than for local news. The consequences may be that high television use may complement high attention to the local community paper in suburbs as well as in outlying areas. Complementary uses may continue to occur; what may change is the mix of specific media that provide complementary as well as competitive functions.

STRUCTURAL IMPLICATIONS FOR THE
CITIZEN INFORMATION ENVIRONMENT

As a determinant of the media environment, community structure influences the use that individuals will make of different media, and their preferences for media as sources of news. As a consequence, the information environment of the average citizen tends to differ sharply from one community to another.

What are the consequences of these differences for level of citizen understanding of public issues and for participation in the processes for deciding these issues? Much of the evidence in the mass communication literature supports the view that participation in public affairs, such as voting, increases as self-exposure to newspaper information rises (Key, 1961; Chaffee, 1975; Kraus and Davis, 1976). However, those findings relate to political participation measured by regularity of voting in national elections; they are generally based upon analysis of individuals within larger national or metropolitan samples. Judging from these data, one might generally expect that interest in public issues would be higher, on the average, in the metropolitan areas where there is heavier circulation of daily newspapers.

There may be a marked difference, however, between average participation over time and involvement in local problems in communities. Participation in the small, less diverse community may appear sporadic and episodic, as a direct result of community structure. That is, small community citizen participation in social action may be more active but less frequent, with activity generally on an issue-specific and personal basis. In urban areas, by contrast, participation in social action may be less active but more frequent and more impersonal, occurring in a more passive way through organized groups.

An additional factor may be the greater deference to the existing power and authorities in the rural communities, which are characterized by a more central elite power structure. Participation there may generally be more nominal, whereas in the urban structure pluralism may result in individuals feeling that through group action they can have greater impacts upon the ultimate decision making. This difference again reflects the greater willingness to compromise in the urban structure and, as indicated earlier in this chapter, a more profound recognition of the plurality of interests and groups, with none of them able to meet all of its goals or achieve all of its ends at any one point in time. This capacity to compromise tends to regulate levels of intensity. The high intensity that often occurs in rural areas may be a result of the community system lacking conflict accommodation systems similar to those in larger and more pluralistic societies.

SUMMARY

Through determining the media environment, community structure has direct influences on citizen use of different media and preferences for them. Typically, in the more tradition-oriented rural community, the local newspaper is a weekly dominated by local news focusing on events other than public affairs. Reading of daily newspapers in such communities is lower than in urban centers which are served by dailies. Television use and preference as a source of news also tends to be higher in the small community than in the urban center. As a result, the public affairs information environment of the small town citizen is substantially more limited than that of the urban citizen.

The entrance of television has led to a changing mix of media available in different communities and, therefore, to different combinations of use that may fit different specializations. Findings from three suburban areas may raise some questions about the view that suburban and center city newspapers complement each other for local citizens. With television providing the highlights of state, national, and international news, suburban citizens may find the daily from a large and nearby city less and less relevant to their community and group concerns. A question for further study is whether television with its news and documentary focus on conflict may in fact be a medium especially attuned to the social problems of a pluralistic society.

NOTES

1. While this question emphasizes the *one* medium most preferred, there were frequently small percentages, usually under 6% or 7%, who nevertheless mentioned two media or more, even following a restatement of the question. Since the overlap is negligible, it was not separated out in this analysis, and preference scores are the *total* percentages in each community mentioning each medium.

2. A question might be raised whether cable television, through expanding offerings or improving reception, might be related to media use and preferences. Since 9 of the 19 communities had cable when studied, the possible influence of cable could be examined. Among two weekly newspaper communities with cable, one was high on daily reading and one was extremely low. All three communities with semiweeklies had cable and all were low on daily reading. They were also low on television viewing and tended to be intermediate on newspaper preference. Only among daily newspaper communities did cable appear to make a difference. Four of the six had cable and were lowest of the daily newspaper group on daily newspaper reading while being highest on television use. But they were high on newspaper preference while varying across the range on television preference. Having a cable system, then, appeared to be unrelated to media *preferences*, although it may be related to use of media in communities having dailies.

REFERENCES

BENSON, L. (1973) "Group cohesion and social and ideological conflict." American Behavioral Scientist 16.

BLAU, P. M. (1975) Parameters of Social Structure: Approaches to the Study of Social Structure. New York: Macmillan.

BOGART, L. (1975) "The future of the metropolitan daily." Journal of Communication 25(2): 30-43.

——— and F. ORENSTEIN (1965) "Mass media and community identity in an interurban setting." Journalism Quarterly 42: 179-188.

CAMPBELL, D. (1970) "A four variable theory of pluralism in American communities." University of Washington Journal of Sociology 2.

CARTER, R. and B. GREENBERG (1964) "Newspapers or television: who do you believe?" Presented at the Association for Education in Journalism Convention, Austin, Texas.

CHAFFEE, S. [ed.] (1975) Political Communication: Issues and Strategies for Research. Beverly Hills, CA: Sage.

––– and D. WILSON (1976) "Media rich, media poor: two studies of diversity in agenda-holding." Presented to the Association for Education in Journalism, College Park, Maryland.

CLARKE, P. and E. FREDIN (1978) "Newspapers, television, and political reasoning." Public Opinion Quarterly 42: 143-160.

COLEMAN, J. S. (1957) Community Conflict. New York: Macmillan.

DeFLEUR, M. and S. BALL-ROKEACH (1975) Theories of Mass Communication. Skokie, IL: Rand McNally.

DONOHUE, G. A., P. J. TICHENOR, and C. N. OLIEN (1973) "Mass media functions, knowledge and social control." Journalism Quarterly 50: 652-659.

EDELSTEIN, A. and B. SCHULZ (1963) "The weekly newspaper's leadership role as seen by community leaders." Journalism Quarterly 40: 565-574.

An Extended View of Public Attitudes Toward Television and Other Mass Media (1977). New York: Television Information Office.

FINIFTER, A. W. and P. R. ABRAMSON (1975) "City size and feelings of political competence." Public Opinion Quarterly 39: 189-198.

GERBNER, G. and L. GROSS (1976) "Living with television: the violence profile." Journal of Communication 26: 173-199.

GREENBERG, B. S. and B. DERVIN (1967) Communication and Related Behaviors of a Sample of Low-Income Urban Adults Compared with a General Population Sample (Project CUP Report 1). East Lansing: Michigan State University.

JANOWITZ, M. (1952) The Community Press in an Urban Setting. New York: Macmillan.

KEY, V. O. (1961) Public Opinion and American Democracy. New York: Knopf.

KRAUS, S. and D. DAVIS (1976) The Effects of Mass Communication on Political Behavior. University Park: Pennsylvania State University Press.

MEIER, R. (1962) A Communications Theory of Urban Growth. Cambridge: MIT Press.

Minnesota Newspaper Association (1976) Annual Directory. Minneapolis: Author.

MORRIS, R. and M. REIN (1973) "Emerging patterns in community planning," in R. L. Warren (ed.) Perspectives on the American Community. Skokie, IL: Rand McNally.

MOTT, G. F. (1973) "Communicative turbulence in urban-dynamics-media, education, and planning." Annals of the American Academy of Political and Social Sciences 405.

OLIEN, C. N., G. A. DONOHUE, and P. J. TICHENOR (1968) "The community editor's power and the reporting of conflict." Journalism Quarterly 47: 472-478.

ROBINSON, J. (1967) "World affairs information and mass media exposure." Journalism Quarterly 44: 23-31.

SCHRAMM, W. and S. WADE (1967) Knowledge and the Public Mind. Palo Alto, CA: Stanford University Institute for Communication Research.

STONE, G. C. (1975) "Management resources in community-sized newspapers." Ph.D. dissertation, Syracuse University.

TICHENOR, P. J., A. I. NNAEMEKA, C. N. OLIEN, and G. A. DONOHUE (1976) "Community pluralism and perceptions of television content." Presented at the Association for Education in Journalism Convention, College Park, Maryland, August.

WESTLEY, B. H. and W. SEVERIN (1963) "How Wisconsinites use and appraise their daily newspapers and other media." University of Wisconsin–Madison. (mimeo)

WHITING, L. R. (1976) "Mass media gatekeepers and community development: aspects of role, perceptions, and performance. M.S. thesis, Iowa State University, Ames.

WILSON, J. Q. (1973) "Planning and politics: citizen participation in urban renewal," in R. L. Warren (ed.) Perspectives on the American Community. Skokie, IL: Rand McNally.

4

Community Structure, Newspapers, and Social Control

The ability of mass media such as newspapers to serve as instruments of social control is a recurring theme in American social thought. Many believe newspapers and other media can reinforce if not mold basic values and patterns of behavior. Repeated and highly organized attempts to bring about changes in television programming are a current and visible expression of this belief. Social pressure on media is a cultural universal. Various public figures have frequently said, with considerable popular support, that newspapers and television can destroy American values by giving undue attention to competing value systems of society. Spiro Agnew's objections in 1969 to media coverage of youth protests present just one example of this popular yet controversial theme.

More than fears that media can wreak social havoc underlie such statements. There is an implicit or even explicit belief that newspapers and television can strengthen the tendencies that are socially approved as well as ones that are socially disapproved.

Recent academic attention to the issue has by and large been more supportive than nonsupportive of the popular view that the press is a dynamic force, which is something of a shift in research perspective. From the late 1940s to the mid 1960s, a view widely expressed in mass communication literature was that media effects are minimal (Lazarsfeld, Berelson and Gaudet, 1948; Katz and Lazarsfeld, 1955; Klapper, 1960; Key, 1961). This view was based to a considerable extent on two kinds of evidence. One is evidence of audience selectivity in self-exposure and interpretation of content. A frequent finding is the tendency of individuals to expose themselves to media reports that are largely congenial to prior dispositions (Berelson and Steiner, 1964). Furthermore, if individuals are somehow confronted with information that does not agree with their prior views, they often tend to rationalize or distort the information in ways that may leave their initial views relatively unscathed (Hyman and Sheatsley, 1947; Festinger, 1957). The voting studies of the Columbia research group were often cited in support of the self-*exposure* hypothesis. Research on information campaigns and on reaction to antiprejudice campaigns seemed to support the selective *interpretation* hypothesis. Concentrated academic attention to "homeostatic" theories of individual cognitive response also tended to support the selective interpretation hypothesis (Maccoby and Maccoby, 1961).

Recent evidence does not reject the principle of individual selectivity, but supports a conclusion quite different from what had come to be viewed as a "minimal effects" perspective about media influence. Clinical evidence several decades ago indicated that comic books may have an impact on child behavior which was generally considered socially undesirable (Wertham, 1952). Results from studies on television impact indicate that under some conditions viewers may be more likely to act out aggressive impulses after viewing aggressive acts on television (Comstock, 1971). This effect, according to at least one study, may accumulate with years of viewing or may show up several years after the viewing itself occurred (Lefkowitz, Eron, Walder, and Huesmann, 1971). Conversely, a few studies have demonstrated that children may be more likely to behave in terms of socially accepted norms after viewing programs that the experimenters termed prosocial (Stein and Friedrich, 1971).

Another body of research has emphasized the role of newspapers and television in the process of focusing the attention of the American public on specific issues. In these "agenda setting" studies, McCombs and Shaw (1972; Shaw and McCombs, 1977) have noted that the ranking of topics in newspapers, according to coverage and display, correlates with readers' ranking of the importance of topics.

It is not clear from these agenda setting studies whether newspapers are in fact *setting* agendas or are reflecting the definitions of important issues that already exist in the public. But whether the media create new patterns of belief or reinforce existing definitions, they are exercising a major social control function. Whether it is by choice or force of circumstances, the selective attention by media to different topics tends to reinforce certain values and norms in society. Evidence from the "gatekeeping" tradition illustrates how some of these controls occur and how they relate to media structures and to individual characteristics of media professions (Gieber, 1964; Donohew, 1967). Breed's (1958) secondary interpretation of studies which he termed a "reverse content analysis" concluded that American newspapers tend to omit economic news and information, particularly if the information may be seen as adverse to the commercial sector. In his frequently cited earlier work, Breed (1955) contended that one of the prime mechanisms for maintaining patterns of selective reporting is the structure of informal relationships in the newsrooms. Without ever being told what "official policy" of the newspaper is regarding different local issues and institutions, Breed found that (1) a widely shared definition of that policy exists among the reporting staff and that (2) through the informal structure, new staffers learn about that definition quickly from their peers and immediate supervisors. Newspaper policy can also be direct and explicit, as Stark (1962) found in a case study. In that situation, the publishers frequently stated their preferences for news coverage, including political views and institutions. Donohew (1967) gathered extensive data on newspaper reporting and editorializing on medicare in Kentucky. He concluded that publisher attitude is a powerful predictor of both content and editorial direction and that attention and posture on the issue were not related to the manifest poverty conditions of the newspapers' coverage areas.

In fact, Donohew's expectation that newspapers would reflect poverty conditions is not in line with a structural hypothesis. The perspective used here would lead to the hypothesis that newspapers will reflect the power structure and the concerns of the community structure. The saying that "newspapers mirror the society" does not mean that they give an accurate reflection of people's needs, but that they mirror the conditions of that system, including power conditions, and power alignments. This point has been made by Breed (1958) in an analysis of economic issues, with negative commercial implications *not* reported by papers.

Reporters and other professional journalists sometimes express their beliefs about the potential influence of media owners' and publishers' views on newspaper content. In early 1979, John Cowles, Jr., owner of the Minneapolis *Star and Tribune,* made several public statements in strong support of a controversial proposal to build a domed stadium in Minneapolis. At one point, a group of reporters on the Minneapolis *Tribune* sponsored an advertisement, in the Minneapolis newspaper and others as well, objecting to the fact that Mr. Cowles was making such statements. In the ad, the reporters stated that "Our role is to report, not participate in, these issues . . . our professional principles have not been undermined by Cowles' involvement in the stadium issue." The ad stated that no executives, including Cowles, had tried to influence coverage, but nevertheless concluded that "to prevent an appearance of such a conflict of interest, we believe management should avoid a leadership role in sensitive political and economic issues" (Minnesota Daily, 1979).

The Minneapolis example demonstrates the difficulty of differentiating the roles of owners, reporters, and editors—all part of an interdependent social subsystem. Independence of these roles requires a conscious and deliberate separation of these roles by members of the subsystem, as well as by members of related social subsystems. For example, when Cowles or other officers occupying similar positions make statements on social issues, they must make it clear that they are speaking in their role as private citizens, and not in their roles as owners or publishers of newspapers. It is equally important that the public understand that the individual is playing different roles at different times. Why should a publisher of a newspaper be subject to censorship of a position taken as a private citizen any more than other newspaper employees or other participants in the system? The classical illustration of this issue is the Hatch Act and the question of its infringements on political participation by federal employees.

SOCIAL CONTROL THROUGH INFORMATION CONTROL

While newspapers and other media have traditionally served as instruments of social control, what is increasingly apparent about this function is that it is based upon distributive control of knowledge. "Knowledge is power" has become a common expression, but less well appreciated is that *control* of knowledge rather than possession or generation of it is central to development and maintenance of a social power base. The growing importance of information control can be seen on a national level, in the size and scope of what Machlup (1962) calls the "knowledge industry," accounting for roughly a fourth of the gross national product. Large-scale organizations are carefully structured to control both the assimilation and the dissemination of information. Professional specialists in modern corporate structures are integrated into a configuration of organized intelligence which is often beyond the comprehension or concern of any one individual (Galbraith, 1967; McDermott, 1969).

Newspapers make up one part of the knowledge industry and have their own specialized functions in control of information. The term *control* is carefully chosen. It refers to continuous and/or routine decision making about whether and how information will be generated and processed and whether and how it will be distributed. During any given day, reporters and editors make a series of such decisions. They may decide whether to cover the city council, ignore it, or run an item based on the minutes brought into the newspaper office by the council secretary. They may decide whether to run a front-page picture of a local civic leader charged with tax fraud or relegate the story to five or six column inches on page 12. They may decide whether and how to set up a headline warning citizens that higher property taxes are in store for next year. And when they are down to the last 10 column inches on the first page, they may find themselves choosing between a story about a youth leader who won a trip to Washington, D.C., and a report of the high school football team's stunning upset of its traditional rival in the next city.

Occasionally, the control aspects of newspaper functioning in a community are made explicit. In a 1977 conference in Minneapolis, a law professor led a discussion of a hypothetical case involving whether newspapers ought to report a 35-year-old incident that could destroy the career of an exemplary local citizen. In discussing this case with an editor, the professor asked if the editor were merely a conduit of news. The editor replied that his paper makes some choices about what facts are pertinent so as to give the story perspective. The following exchange then ensued:

Professor: Then instead of being a conduit, you act as a filter . . . you engage in censorship then.

Editor (smiling): We call it editing.

Professor: When a judge does it [issues a restraining order] you call it prior restraint; when *you* do it, you call it editing.[1]

Such decisions about information have control consequences in proportion to social dependence upon that information. DeFleur and Ball-Rokeach (1975, 1976) have pointed out various forms of dependency, ranging from the need to find the best buys in groceries to the need to maintain contact with the world outside the neighborhood and to the desire to escape the tensions of everyday life. Dependency upon mass media for information generally increases as society becomes more complex. The greater this dependency, the greater the likelihood that decisions about information control will have consequences for the individual and collective lives of the community. However, this dependency is itself a product of prior information control. Professional groups, as one illustration, develop specialized languages and jargon that are intelligible only to other professional sepcialists. These specialized languages are control mechanisms which leave client groups in a state of dependency upon a professional group which is often limited to authorized or licensed persons who dispense the information.

INFORMATION CONTROL AND COMMUNITY CONFLICT

Among the various decisions which newspapers make about information, perhaps none leads to as much concern among reporters and editors as decisions about reporting the disagreements, clashes, and confrontations in local public life. Gatekeepers may themselves be under pressure from contesting powers; to whom shall they bow? Although social conflict historically has been a major ingredient of news in the community (Lippmann, 1963), the reporting of conflict may be subject to a variety of spoken and unspoken rules. In the Chicago urban area, Janowitz (1952) found the community press putting some sharp limits on the reporting of controversy, limits which could not be explained by the particular format, scope, or subject matter of the community paper.

Citizen responses to Janowitz's queries reflect close identification of the community press with the community as a whole. Respondents perceived the newspaper as they might perceive any business or agency in the community. That is, they saw the newspaper as developing community spirit, as encouraging growth of community facilities, and as aiding everyday life and commerce—all facets of community maintenance. They did not, however, see the community newspaper as a forum for concentrating on social debates or divisions.

Why does the community press so frequently downplay social and political conflict? Janowitz explained that the community newspaper is generally seen by its audience as neither political nor partisan, but rather as an agent of community welfare and progress. While many of the papers studied by Janowitz favored political candidates in subtle ways, they avoided editorializing almost completely and devoted 1% or less of news content to explicitly partisan activities even during an election period. Kearl (1951) found a sample of Wisconsin weeklies giving somewhat greater coverage to politics during the height of the 1940 election campaign, but still under 10% of nonadvertising content. This type of political reporting appears to serve as a kind of socially acceptable ritual that does not involve a contest and, therefore, does not lead to intense conflict.

Similarly, in a community case study, Edelstein and Schulz (1963) documented small community leaders' criticisms of the conflict content of the local newspaper as a threat to community structure and values. In a Minnesota study (Olien, Donohue, and Tichenor, 1968) more than half (59%) of the weekly papers reported no local governmental conflict of any kind during a one-month study period. In contrast, 80% of the daily newspapers in the study reported some aspect of local governmental conflict during the same period of study. When communities were analyzed according to size, a third of the papers in towns under 3,500 reported conflict in the study period, compared with two-thirds in those places with population over 3,500. Similarly, Hvistendahl (1970) found weeklies less aggressive than twice-weekly papers in getting information from public records in their communities.

Although differences between small town and metropolitan papers in reporting conflict may reflect differences in structure, reporting of it in *either* place is a form of conflict control. The "rules of the game" that apply in reporting conflict—such as the ritualistic political reporting that Kearl found, letters to editors, and reliance on official documents—are all attempts to channel conflict so that it will be less disruptive of the existing system.

TWO PROCESSES OF CONTROL

The pattern of quiescent reporting of public affairs, which is characteristic of community newspapers, may be viewed within a functional perspective of information control. In this perspective, newspapers may fulfill community maintenance functions by two sets of processes which, while different, do overlap. They are *feedback control* and *distribution control* processes.

Feedback, is a term used in an inclusive way, with media treated as subsystems which provide a feedback or "regulatory" function for other components of the social system, or for the total system itself. The feedback-control function of mass media finds both its empirical basis and its philosophical expression in the historic conception of the fourth estate or "watchdog" role of the press. Newspaper reporting of debates in the city council, challenges to the school board, labor-management strife, and consumer protests about supermarket prices are all examples of feedback-control. Through reporting the dvisions in the society, the newspaper draws attention to problems. By focusing attention, that is, setting agendas for public discussion on social issues, the media are serving a feedback or regulatory function in the system sense of the term. Newspapers and other media do not direct the course of action which may follow once the problem has been identified; their function is a more limited one of shaping the public's definitions of what the real issue is. Newspaper reporting of social problems might be compared, in a crude analogy, to a thermostat which signals a change in temperature level, thereby triggering an activation of the system without determining a specific response by the heating and air conditioning unit. It should be added that the thermostat itself is not an independent mechanism since it can be set high or low; analogously, the power structure of a community determines, in part, the setting of the thermostat.

Distribution control, which can occur either independently or jointly with feedback-control, serves a maintenance function but in a different way. Here, the control is based on selective dissemination and a wide variety of distributional techniques as well as selective withholding of information. "Distributive" information is that which is received and acted upon without necessarily requiring any further communication back to the newspaper or to any other major institutions. If distributive information stimulates social contact, it is largely at the informal, personal, and friendship levels. News reports about club meetings, charity basaars, availability of disaster aid application forms, and schedules of church events are acts of distribution control by the newspapers, no matter how routine these reports may be. Reports on government may be purely distribution control to the extent that such reports are limited to notices of meetings and reports of actions that require no citizen reaction to institutions, such as notices of snow plowing schedules and road repairs.

Generally speaking, then, distributive information is for routine consumption; and feedback information has the potential for stimulating individual or organized reaction or protest. Yet, the two classes of information may occur together, even in the same message. A report about last night's council meeting may contain both distributive information (about where to buy tags for pets) and feedback information (about a confrontation between the mayor and a councilman over the tag requirement or price). Some information may serve a purely distributive function for one individual or group and a feedback-control function for another, i.e., information may function differently for various parts of the community.

NEWSPAPER TYPE AND FUNCTIONS

Evidence to date generally supports the hypothesis that the less complex and differentiated the community, the more likely the newspaper in that community is to confine itself to the distributive aspect of information control. Also, there is support for the related hypothesis that the more complex and pluralistic the community, the more likely the newspaper is to perform a feedback as well as a distributive function. Yet, in either case, the distributive function may well be far and away the most frequently performed of the two functions.

Evidence for these hypotheses appears in a variety of studies. To the extent that Janowitz (1952) was dealing with newspapers of relatively homogeneous segments (suburbs) of the total metropolis, his findings about the content of community papers are largely in line with these hypotheses. Homogeneous communities, viewing the newspaper as an extension of personal communication and having fewer mechanisms for protecting the social order against disruption, may well look to the press as an instrument for prevention and suppression of tension. Such factors would assign a quite different role in reporting social action, to these papers as opposed to metropolitan papers, and that role may be widely agreed upon within the community. Two-thirds of the small town leaders which Edelstein and Schulz (1963) interviewed said newspapers should publish controversy "only when it could not avoid doing so." Those responses came from leaders in a place with 3,600 population.

Edelstein and Schulz compared responses of their leaders with responses from 41 publishers of Washington papers whom they termed "journalist-editors," and therefore *most* likely to express traditional journalist ethics. However, when asked about the newspaper's role in handling local controversial activities, barely half (51%) of the journalist-editors agreed that "The weekly newspaper should take the initiative in publicizing controversies," a statement that generally reflects a basic part of the tradition of journalism. Agreement with that statement was even lower (32%) among the leaders, although the difference between the two groups was not statistically significant.

The authors did not regard the journalist-editor as necessarily typical; they reported estimates by Shaw and Irwin that the proportion of weekly newspaper editors expressing journalist-editor ideology at that time was no more than one of five. Even in that group, such editors were thought by the authors to act rarely on such ideology. More common, they concluded, was the "community editor" role, concerned with maintaining spirit, harmony, and consensus, printing "only those facts that stressed the good points of the community."

The data reported by Edelstein and Schulze (1963) were from different sources and did not include comparisons by community type. Such comparisons were made in a 1965 Minnesota study of editors of 54 weeklies and 34 twice-weeklies and dailies (Olien, Donohue, and Tichenor, 1968). In this study, editors were asked, "What, in your opinion, are some of the main things your newspaper does for the community?" Responses were grouped in six categories (Table 4-1). For these editors, the information function (distributive) was paramount, with promotion of local business and civic life holding a strong second place. On these characteristics, editors of papers in all types of communities were very much alike.

On three other characteristics, however, some clear differences support the proposition that papers in different kinds of communities have different functions. Compared with editors of twice-weeklies and dailies, the weekly editors were more likely (24% versus 9%) to make a statement that fell into the "development-of-community-identity" category. On the other hand, the editors of larger papers were *more* likely than weekly editors to mention opinion leadership and education (44% versus 26%) and interest arousal (26% versus 11%).

Most of these editors, however, saw themselves as primarily reporters of the local scene and promoters of civic and economic sectors of community life. And although editors of larger papers were more likely to give responses that could be classified as feedback control functions, only 3 editors among the entire 88 referred specifically to the "watchdog-over-govern-

Table 4-1 Editors' Views of "Some of the Main Things the Newspaper Does for This Community" (in percent)

	Weeklies	Twice-weeklies & Dailies
Provides news, information	76	68
Business and civic promotion	50	53
Advertising	26	18
Development of community identity (self-image, "mirror of community")	24	9[*]
Provides opinion leadership, education	26	44[*]
Interest arousal	11	26[*]

[*]$p < .05$, one-tail

ment" role that is so prominent in historical accounts of American journalism. Only 2 made explicit mentions of controversy or conflict and 1 of these qualified his statement by saying that, nevertheless, his intent was to "put our best foot forward."

It might be pointed out that the 1965 study was conducted during a time (early in the American involvement in the Vietnam conflict) when there was growing state and federal agency involvement in rural areas development. There had not been a high degree of community-wide arousal of either a supportive *or* adversary type, although leadership groups in some counties had reacted sharply to designations, based on union and economic data, as "underdeveloped." The environmental issue, the energy issue, and political regionalization were largely questions for the future. A current survey of editors of the same newspapers might well tap a greater degree of reporting and greater acting out of the watchdog role, especially as it relates to distant government.[2] There is also the possibility of increased emphasis on investigative reporting among professional journalists generally, following Watergate and the wide attention given to the role of journalists in that episode. Since newspapers reflect the topical concerns of the time and the particular techniques for dealing with them, the concerns of newspapers change in accordance with community concerns.

Reports of conflict may increasingly become unavoidable in the small community press since conflict frequently exists in a wide area and gets attention on television and in other media. But when such an eventuality occurs, there is a high likelihood that the conflict will be reported in a way that minimizes local differences. This happened in 3 of the 19 Minnesota community studies, when crisis situations developed as a result of actions initiated by external agencies and metropolitan media circulating in the local community reported them. In that kind of situation, the editor often reports the crisis in spite of wishes to the contrary. In the midst of the power-line controversy of 1975-1977, a weekly editor in one community said in an editorial:

Because of the power line dispute, [this] county has suddenly become a mecca for [metropolitan] newsmen. . . . When [this town] went to the state basketball tournament . . . the publicity was paltry compared to the current flood of radio, TV and newspaper coverage. Our regret is that the coverage reports a very divisive event. We wish it could have recorded a happier or more popular happening.

HOW CITIZENS VIEW COMMUNITY DECISION MAKING

The similarities in views between leaders and editors on the part played by newspapers in the community are not peculiar to journalistic performance alone. Rather, the differences in perceptions between editors in larger and smaller communities as well as among other groups should be regarded as part of a more general structural difference between such places.

Theoretically, any social system is basically a series of interdependent control mechanisms. The newspaper is one of those mechanisms, but only one. Another mechanism is the existing pattern of attitudes and values. Just as the newspaper in a smaller community operates on a consensus basis, so might the general public perceive decision making in a small community, compared with a larger one, as involving a small number of persons and agencies and a high degree of consensus about the decisions that are made.

Some data relevant to this proposition were gathered in 1973 and 1974 in the four "metal industry" communities. Respondents in these communities were asked to assume that, "a major decision had to be made affecting water quality in rivers, lakes and city water around here." They were then asked a series of questions about (1) whether a small or large number of persons would be expected to take part in the decision, (2) whether one or two or whether many government organizations or agencies would take part, (3) whether they expected much attention to be given to public opinion before the decision was made, and (4) whether they expected a great deal of community agreement on such decisions.

The results (Table 4-2) are generally in line with the structural hypothesis that citizens in more homogeneous commu-

Table 4-2 Perceptions of Public Decision Making in Four Communities, 1972 and 1974

| | Smaller, more homogeneous communities | | | | | Larger urban community | |
| | Community L | | Community J | | Community H* | Community C | |
Suppose a major decision had to be made affecting water quality in rivers, lakes and city water around here. Would you:	'72	'74	'72	'74	'72	'72	'74
Percent who							
1. Expect a small number to take part in decision	45	50	31	42	27	36	31
2. Expect only 1 or 2 organizations or government agencies to take part	39	32	31	34	21	24	28
3. Expect much attention to be given to public opinion before final decision	45	48	64	63	70	70	70
4. Expect a great deal of community agreement on decisions like this	42	39	65	67	33	37	36

*Community H was not studied in 1974.

91

nities tend to expect a smaller amount of participation, less attention to public opinion, and more eventual agreement. For each of the four questions about the hypothetical community decision about a water quality decision, differences appear each year between the smallest communities (L and J) and the largest (community C) in the predicted direction. The major exception is community H, studied only in 1972, where perceptions are more like those of the urban center than like those of the smallest communities. On three of the items, small community H responses are more "urban" than those of large community C; on the remaining item the proportion expecting "much attention" to public opinion is identical with that of C. Otherwise, the only difference that does not fit the pluralism hypothesis, is that in 1972, the proportion expecting a "small number to take part" is lower in small community J than in large community C.

In general, the respondents in the two smallest and most homogeneous communities were more likely to expect the decision to be dominated by a small number of persons and organizations, were less likely to expect much attention to public opinion, and were more likely to expect a high level of agreement on the decision.

On the other hand, the deviation of small community H from predictions of the model may be quite important to take into account. Small community H is larger and somewhat more diverse than small communities L or J. Its population (about 8,000) is roughly twice as large as that of community J and about 66% more than community L. However, community H is still less than a tenth the size of large community C. While community H is a regional center with a twice-weekly paper, it is clearly not an urban place according to indicators of pluralism. It is a growing recreational, service, and trade center but has a declining agricultural sector and is developing an increasingly cosmopolitan composition. Its forest industry is large and employs people from the entire county.

These results sugest that pluralism, while associated with numbers of citizens, may be a result of other factors as well. It is possible to have a large concentration of population with relatively little diversity, a phenomenon often observed in developing nations where large population centers may have a decidely rural and homogeneous character. On the other hand, a small community near a diversifying metropolitan center may retain its small size and yet become increasingly urban in occupational patterns and in its general character. Thus, small, older communities once dependent on farming become more urban in character as travel to a nearby large city for work, leisure, and shopping increases.

COMMUNITY STRUCTURE AND CONTROL OF SCIENTIFIC INFORMATION

The structural factors in communities that determine how people picture decision making should, in theory, carry over to their attitudes toward information itself. There are at least two basic values regarding information in the Western democratic tradition, and the degree to which they are held would be expected to vary according to community type. One of these values is that widespread distribution of information is desirable in and of itself. The different but related value is that *use* of specialized knowledge from scientists and other experts aids in attainment of social goals sought by individuals and organized groups, including creation and maintenance of a social power base (Lakoff, 1971).

Theoretically, attitudes toward knowledge within a community should vary along the same lines as attitudes about decision making generally. Attitudes toward the control of knowledge are part of an integrated total system and, from a holistic perspective, can only be understood in the total social context. Compared with residents of more urban, pluralistic communities, one would expect residents of a smaller and more homogeneous community to:

(1) express lower support for mass dissemination of scientific information relevant to public decisions

(2) express lower support for *use* of scientific information in public
decision making.

The first of these propositions rests on principles, already
discussed, about community organization and functioning. Decision making in the smaller community is based largely on
precedent and tradition in an atmosphere of general consensus.
The predictable tendency in such a community is to decrease
the likelihood of social disruption by conducting public affairs
in all institutions at a relatively informal level and managing
conflict by suppression.

Decision making in the larger community necessarily must
take pluralism into account. The process, by the nature of the
structure, is forced to consider the differing and often conflicting interests of the various groups. Among the characteristics of
more pluralistic centers are their greater need for generation and
use of formalized knowledge, as a result of the secondary
formalized relationships among groups. The more complex the
community, the more the interdependencies and the greater the
need for knowledge of other parts by any one segment. Greater
reliance on formal dissemination of knowledge in more heterogeneous social systems has been noted frequently (Benson,
1973). Such a community achieves coordination in different
ways. Compared with more homogeneous communities, the
larger community has more mechanisms for ameliorating conflict as well as for facilitating greater communication among its
parts (Morris and Rein, 1973). Theoretically, attitudes toward
knowledge are at least partly a function of community structure. Attitudes reflect the general recognition of the need for
knowledge in resolving social issues. Some earlier evidence suggests that these differences may extend to a set of attitudes in
the system toward communication in general. Nix and Sheerley
(1973) found that urban respondents were more oriented toward "coordinative" community needs (such as better communication between agencies) than were rural respondents. Whereas the emphasis in an urban center was on coordination and
communication, Nix and Sheerley found rural respondents putting more emphasis on "getting things done." Such findings

support the conclusion that decision making in the small community is oligarchical; "getting things done" is an orientation toward execution of decisions.

The expectation that small town residents would show less support for *use* of scientific information in decision making follows parallel reasoning. The greater the degree of specialization, the more highly valued expert knowledge would tend to become and the higher the status that scientists and other specialists would achieve as legitimizers. How do leaders in a complex, urban area deal with the limitations of their individual knowledge? Largely, it would seem, they do so by seeking out if not depending upon information from recognized experts. Furthermore, those experts are more likely to be around and available, if not actively offering their advice and counsel, in the urban center. Experts and expertise are integral parts of an urban community's mode of accommodating intergroup conflicts. Also, more formalized mechanisms often specify the specific type of expertise necessary for decision making in an urban area—such as legal expertise in a hearing situation. These specifications of expertise themselves serve to mediate and regulate conflict situations.

By contrast, the structure of traditional, homogeneous communities contains mechanisms and conditions which may have a braking effect on use of specialized knowledge. First, they lack the easy access to such knowledge that exists in bigger cities. Also, the high value on local autonomy in traditional communities may be seen as threatened by knowledge from experts, especially if that knowledge originates from agencies outside the existing community structure (Warren, 1973).

Data that bear on these questions are limited to two of the "metal industry group" communities where similar issues had occurred. In both small community L (Population 4,500) and large community C (population 100,000), a heavily publicized debate occurred over application of state and federal pollution control standards relating to local industry. In each, there had been an "industry-versus-environment" dispute, amid conflicting interpretations of scientific evidence on the alleged environmental hazards of the respective industrial operations.

Respondents in these communities were asked a number of items concerning their opinions about scientific information. One set of items was designed to measure support for distribution of scientific information in conflict situations. An illustrative item, with agree-disagree response alternatives, is "scientific information should be held back if it looks like it might lead to public disagreement in the community." Another set of items measured perceived worth of scientific information for use in decision making. An example agree-disagree item is "People would trust government more if public decisions depended more on scientific information."

COMMUNITY STRUCTURE AND PUBLIC SUPPORT

Data (Table 4-3) are consistent with the proposition that public support for mass dissemination of scientific information will be higher in the more pluralistic, heterogeneous community. Overall differences between communities, based on scale averages, are significant ($p < .01$) for 1974; for 1972, the difference is in the predicted direction but is nonsignificant statistically ($p > .05$).

While there are differences between the large and small community, the differences observed between communities is in *degree* of public support. In each case, a majority supports dissemination even when the information is explicitly assumed to produce public controversy. Such support is interesting in view of recent increases in public skepticism about scientific *institutions*. Whatever they may think about science leaders and agencies, the data here and in LaPorte and Metlay's (1975) research indicate that members of the U.S. public continue to place a high value on widespread availability of scientific results. This is a characteristic running through Western industrial democracies and might not be found in other societies that rely less on scientific development and specialized information.

Results are also consistent with the proposition that public support for use of scientific information in public decision making will be higher in the more heterogeneous community.

Table 4-3 Perceived Support for Distribution of Scientific Information in a Conflict Situation, Among Public Samples in Two Communities, 1972 and 1974 (illustrative items)

	1972		1974	
	Small Community L (N = 102)	Large Community C (N = 131)	Small Community L (N = 101)	Large Community C (N = 134)
Scientific information should be held back if it looks like it might lead to public disagreement in the community (percent who disagree)	77	85	80	87
A wide open public debate about environmental problems is healthy for this community (percent who agree)	82	90	85	90
The way things have gone at the Metro City factory, it might have been better if we had never heard those scientific reports about pollution (percent who disagree)	64	75	55	84
If scientific evidence of pollution leads to more public disagreements like the one at Regional City, it might be better not to report that evidence (percent who disagree)	77	84	80	87
Total Scale Score[a]	18.93	19.47[b]	18.85	19.73[c]

a. 7– item total scale, maximum score of 21, scored so that a higher score reflects higher support for distribution of scientific information.
b. (Community difference, $p > .05, < .10$
c. Difference, $p < .01$.

Table 4-4 Perceived Worth of Scientific Information for Use in Decision Making in Two Communities, 1972 and 1974 (illustrative items)

	1972		1974	
	Small Community L (N = 102)	Large Community C (N = 101)	Small Community L (N = 131)	Large Community C (N = 134)
People would trust government more if public decisions depended more on scientific information (percent who agree)	54	62	59	70
In solving an air of water pollution problem, there is no substitute for knowing the scientific facts (percent who agree)	71	76	65	77
Scientists often confuse things by telling us more than we need to know to solve a problem (percent who disagree)	45	61	60	72
There is too much information given out by scientists on problems (percent who disagree)	70	78	75	85
The drug problem is an example of people learning more scientific information than is good for them (percent who disagree)	64	77	68	74
Total Scale Score[a]	23.17	24.79[b]	24.46	26.05[b]

a. 11 – item total scale, maximum score of 33, scored so that a higher score reflects higher worth of scientific information.

b. Community difference, p < .01.

Again, consistent differences in the predicted direction exist between communities (Table 4-4). Differences based on scale averages are significant ($p < .01$) for both years. Also, as in the previous table, majorities make the positive response on most items, with the difference being largely in magnitude rather than direction.

There is one further piece of evidence supporting this proposition. An underlying assumption is that residents of these communities differentially perceive actual use of scientific information in making decisions. As a check on that assumption, respondents were asked whether public leaders today depend more, less, or about the same on scientific information. In each year, a higher proportion of respondents in the urban city said more; the proportions were 59% and 74% for the small community (L) and the large community (C), respectively, in 1972 and 59% and 68% in 1974.

LEADERS AND PUBLICS

If respondents of a more homogeneous community place a lower value on support and use of scientific information and expect higher agreement on public decisions generally, one might predict that those residents would agree more with their leaders. That is, agreement between leaders and the general public on both dissemination and use of scientific information would be greater in the more homogeneous community.

To test these expectations, community leaders in both the small community (L) and the large community (C) were chosen through a reputational procedure modified to identify persons known to be directly involved in the local environmental issue.[3] In each case, an initial contact was made with a public agency staff member known to be highly familiar with the local issue. Persons named as involved by that informant were interviewed and asked to name others who were active.

Findings, however, are quite contrary to the hypothesis that leader-public agreement on dissemination and use of information will be higher in the smaller town. Leaders in the smaller

Table 4-5 Leader and Public Opinion Scores on Distribution and Use of Scientific Information in Two Communities

	Community L			Community C		
	Leaders (N = 25)	1972 Public (N = 102)	1974 Public (N = 101)	Leaders (N = 24)	1972 Public (N = 131)	1974 Public (N = 134)
Average scale score, support distribution of scientific information in a conflict situation[a]	20.08	18.93	18.85	20.16	19.47	19.73
Difference between leaders and combined public samples	1.16	(leaders higher)		.56	(leaders higher)	
Average scale score, perceived worth of scientific information for use in decision-making[b]	26.64	23.17	24.46	24.83	24.79	26.05
Difference between leaders and combined public samples	2.93	(leaders higher)		-.60	(public higher)	

a. 7 – item scale, maximum score = 21, higher score means more support.
b. 11 – item scale, maximum score = 33, higher score means higher perceived worth.

community tend to express nearly as much support for distribution of information and higher perceived worth of scientific information as their community C counterparts (Table 4-5). Consequently, there is a *wider* difference between leaders and public in the small community than in the large community C, which is directly contrary to the pluralism hypothesis. For several items, support for distribution was nearly universal among leaders of both communities. For example, all except one leader in both communities disagreed with holding scientific information back "if it looks as if it might create controversy."

These findings are similar in a major respect to results from a Georgia study. Nix and Sheerley (1973) found that urban adults, compared with rural adults, expressed more of a "coordinative" orientation that stressed negotiation and intergroup communication. These investigators also found that leaders in both kinds of communities express a higher degree of coordinative orientation than nonleaders, while leader groups themselves did not differ significantly from one community to the other. In terms of percentage points, the leader-public difference reported by Nix and Sheerley in their rural community was more than twice as great as in their urban community.

LEADERS AND PUBLICS: A DIFFERENT SET OF DRUMS?

These findings suggest that on the question of using expert information, community publics and their leaders may be marching to the beat of different drums. Leaders, like professionals generally, are in many ways marginal members of the local community. They are links between the local community and the larger society, as Vidich and Bensman (1968) observe. So while community structure may partially determine public views about distributing and using scientific information, leader views on that information may arise from a more complex set of circumstances. With growing numbers of governmental agencies that the community must deal with, corporations seeking (or being sought for) locations in the community, leaders may be among the first to recognize the crucial nature of specialized information. The leaders studied here were, by study design, those involved in environmental decisions. That experience itself may have brought home the value of having access to scientists or the results of science in dealing with such vexing problems as deciding whether to mine in a wilderness area. Leaders, however, are not necessarily completely neutral, even initially, on such questions. They may have a preferred resolution or a position to which they are publicly committed. Would such a preference or commitment make scientific information irrelevant? Quite the contrary: Expert information may become a formidable resource if not a decisive weapon in making the case that the leader must make in defending or advocating the position to which he or she is committed.

At the same time that small town leaders are highly predisposed to accept scientific knowledge, they may be even *more* optimistic than their urban counterparts about the outcome of science in decision making. In response to another question, the small town leaders were more likely to state that in addition to using technical information from scientists, decision makers should *depend* to a great extent on what scientists recommend. It is also likely that small town structure tends to produce more of an appeal to scientific authori*ty*, whereas the urban structure leads more to concern with authori*ties*. This line of reasoning is supported by responses to the item "Scientists disagree among themselves as much as politicians do." Among the 24 urban leaders, 87% agreed, compared with 56% of the small town leaders. That finding suggests that the urban leaders are indeed more attuned to the potentially conflicting nature of scientific evidence and testimony. They were not opposed to scientific information; none said it should be ignored. But in perceiving more disagreement among scientists, the urban leaders may well have demonstrated a more realistic perception of how scientists as a professional grouping behave.

SUMMARY

Among the social controls that maintain the norms, values, and processes of a community, those that regulate the generation and distribution of information are some of the most pervasive. Newspapers are highly visible mechanisms of this type and, as such, their functions necessarily fit into a pattern that varies predictably according to size and type of community.

In a larger sense, weeklies and dailies may be seen as part of the same overall system, but as components of differential power structures to which they respond. That power structure may be pluralistic or monolithic, where consensus reporting is a function of a monolithic local structure and reporting conflicting ideas and actions is yielding to a plurality of powers in diverse sectors, which may be in conflict only in limited areas and at specific times.

Newspaper decisions about information can be seen as being of two basically different types, feedback control and distribution control. The former includes decisions about information that alerts the total system about activities or characteristics of other parts, with the potential for stimulating reactive communication or other action. The latter, distribution control, deals with information which is primarily for routine consumption.

Evidence from a number of sources generally supports some basic propositions about the employment of these information control mechanisms in different kinds of communities. The structural characteristic which has been examined in most detail is the extent to which the community is small and homogeneous, with a pattern of decision making by tradition and precedent, rather than urban, large, and heterogeneous. To the extent that a community is homogeneous, these tendencies exist:

(1) a greater emphasis in newspaper content on purely distributive rather than feedback information, in the interest of maintaining an atmosphere of consensus and serene tranquillity

(2) a greater likelihood that community editors themselves will support the newspaper's emphasis on distributive information, thereby agreeing more closely with community leadership generally

(3) a correspondingly greater belief among citizens that decisions in the community are both (a) made by a small number of persons and (b) widely agreed upon within the community once they are made

(4) a lesser degree of support in the public at large for widespread

dissemination of expert scientific information and for use of that information in public decision making

(5) a potentially greater difference between public and leaders on whether scientific information should be widely distributed or used in public decision making.

Such observed tendencies toward maintenance of consensus and surface harmony in the smaller community do not guarantee that the community press will *never* deal with controversy; rather, the homogeneous community structure provides a continuing pressure against such controversy. With increasing entrance of new and stronger external forces into the community, however, the role of the community press may differ, as it did in the power-line issue. The community press in these cases, however, will often portray a community relatively unified in its concerns or in its opposition to the outside force. However, once an issue erupts, the community press may at least temporarily give as much attention to the scope, tension, and bitterness of the conflict as a metropolitan newspaper might—perhaps even more so.[4]

There are at least two aspects of community newspaper coverage of conflict that are open for further study. One is the question of whether reporting of internal divisions, when it does occur, is followed by periods of "consensus" reporting which may serve a healing function and a restoration of the image of harmony. Another, and related, question is whether the increasing level of training among journalists is itself producing a greater amount of feedback reporting (Johnstone, Bowman, and Slawski, 1976). To the extent that such is the case, and increases in conflict reporting stem from more education and a greater sense of professionalism among journalists, the reporting of public issues might become a more regular and routine feature of the community press, rather than something that comes in spurts followed by therapeutic periods of consensus-reporting. These are important questions for the journalistic professions and for consideration by community leadership as well.

NOTES

1. While the emphasis here is on communication control decisions within news-papers themselves, it must be acknowledged (as the editor-professor exchange indi-cates) that newspapers are frequently subject to control by other agencies, and the exertion of such control will not always be as publicly visible as the judicial restraining order. As this book was being written, a proposal to locate a large landfill for chemical waste in Minnesota was under strong citizen opposition, and newspaper articles were suggesting that the issue might take on characteristics similar to the power line controversy. In the landfill issue, one early point of contention was a proposal from a public relations firm to handle the pollution control agency's public information and education program. According to a newspaper report, the proposal initially included the following statements:

> We will want [news-media] coverage from a perspective favorable to the [landfill project]. . . . This will be a hot issue and we will have to guide the press away from making it an emotionally explosive one. . . . The obvious danger . . . is that [the landfill] is a natural newsmaker, which if left unattended can run amuck, taking on a momentum of its own, overrunning the public-information program objectives. Carefully controlled release of information and precise coordination between all efforts and departments is essential.

2. It might also be added that new forms of community journalism, specifically neighborhood newspapers, may produce a somewhat different pattern of editor perception of newspaper functions. Ward and Gaziano (1976) interviewed editors or coordinators of 13 neighborhood newspapers and 10 newsletters in the Minneapolis-St. Paul metropolitan area, all of which circulate to households within specific urban neighborhoods and cover a fairly broad spectrum of local news. They asked a question similar to the one from the 1965 study of Minnesota community newspaper editors and found a quite different pattern of answers. The most frequent responses were classified by the authors as "Informs community about itself" (mentioned by 74%) and "Develops community identity and pride" (mentioned by 61%). Also, Ward and Gaziano found four editors who said one of their chief jobs was to "communicate with outside decision-makers." These authors concluded that most of the urban neighborhood editors view their roles as activist, particularly in contro-versies that might involve the neighborhood and decision makers at the county level. And while they saw little tendency for the neighborhood editors to be protective of any institution, they point out that these papers deal with few strictly neighborhood institutions having much formal political power. Therefore, editors may seek greater neighborhood cohesiveness by reporting conflicts between the neighborhood and outside decision makers. As with the rural town weeklies reporting the power line controversy, drawing attention to conflict between local and outside interests may enhance the development of local identity. Furthermore, by *concentrating* on the outside forces, the community or neighborhood paper in a heated controversy may in fact draw attention away from sharp internal divisions that may well accompany such issues.

3. In terms of methodology for identifying members of power structures, this

approach represents a combination of *reputational* and *decision* procedures (see Aiken, 1970).

4. The power-line issue in the most recent community studies is not the only one in which the role of the community press has differed sharply from its usual consensus-oriented role. When new and external forces bring a new issue into the community, the community press may temporarily employ reporting procedures that portray the full dimensions of the controversy, including the acrimony and rancor that may be generated within the community itself. An example is a county seat weekly paper's reporting of a 1973 confrontation between the local county board and an organization of local farmers opposed to construction of a new electric power plant in the area. The county board had gone on record supporting the plant as a boost to the local economy; farmers opposed it as harmful to agriculture. The paper's front-page headline said, "Are You with AG or Power Company? Farm Group Asks County Board." The opening sentences of the story below were:

> Opponents to the construction of an electrical generating plant and county commissioners tangled in another shouting match here Tuesday. The verbal fisticuffs, finger-pointing personality barbs erupted during the commissioner's regular meeting in the courthouse attended by some 50 members of [an] organization attempting to halt . . . plans for development of a giant coal-burning generating plant.

The story was framed by a picture of an angry, gesturing farmer on one side of the page and a grimacing, hand-waving commissioner on the other. The article also reported that sheriff's deputies had been asked to attend the meeting and that the farm organization had invited television camera crews from a nearby metropolitan area. The story had received state-wide publicity for several previous weeks.

REFERENCES

AGNEW, S. T. (1969) "Address of Vice-President Spiro T. Agnew to the Midwest Regional Republican Committee." Des Moines, Iowa, November 13.

AIKEN, M. (1970) "The distribution of community power: structural bases and social consequences," in M. Aiken and P. E. Mott (eds.) The Structure of Community Power. New York: Random House.

———— and P. E. MOTT (1970) The Structure of Community Power. New York: Random House.

BENSON, L. (1973) "Group cohesion and social and ideological conflict." American Behavioral Scientist 16.

BERELSON, B. and G. STEINER (1964) Human Behavior: An Inventory of Scientific Findings. New York: Harcourt Brace Jovanovich.

BETHELL, T. (1977) "The myth of an adversary press." Harpers Magazine (January): 33-40.

BREED, W. (1958) "Mass communication and social integration." Social Forces 37: 109-116.

———— (1955) "Social control in the newsroom." Social Forces 33: 323-335.

COMSTOCK, G. A. (1971) "New research on media content and control," in G. A. Comstock and E. Rubinstein (eds.) Television and Social Behavior. Washington, DC: Government Printing Office.

DeFLEUR, M. and S. BALL-ROKEACH (1976) "Dependency model of mass media effects." Communication Research 3, 1.

----- (1975) Theories of Mass Communication. New York: David McKay Co.

DONOHEW, L. (1967) "Newspaper gatekeeper and forces in the news channels." Public Opinion Quarterly 31: 61-68.

EDELSTEIN, A. and B. SCHULZ (1963) "The weekly newspaper's leadership role as seen by community leaders." Journalism Quarterly 40: 565-574.

FESTINGER, L. (1957) A Theory of Cognitive Dissonance. Palo Alto, CA: Stanford University Press.

GALBRAITH, J. K. (1967) The New Industrial State. Boston: Houghton Mifflin.

GIEBER, W. (1964) "News is what newspapermen make it," in L. A. Dexter and D. M. White (eds.) People, Society, and Mass Communication. New York: Macmillan.

HESSE, M. B. and S. H. CHAFFEE (1973) "Coorientation in political communication: a structural analysis." Presented at the meeting of the International Communication Association, Montreal, Canada, April.

HVISTENDAHL, J. K. (1970) "Publisher's power: functional or dysfunctional?" Journalism Quarterly 47: 472-478.

HYMAN, H. H. and P. B. SHEATSLEY (1947) "Some reasons why information campaigns fail." Public Opinion Quarterly 11: 413-423.

JANOWITZ, M. (1952) The Community Press in an Urban Setting. New York: Macmillan.

JOHNSTONE, J.W.C., E. W. SLAWSKI, and W. W. BOWMAN (1976) The News People: A Sociological Portrait of American Journalists and Their Work. Urbana: University of Illinois Press.

KATZ, E. and P. LAZARSFELD (1955) Personal Influence. New York: Macmillan.

KEARL, B. E. (1951) "Content of Wisconsin newspapers during selected election periods." Ph.D. dissertation. Minneapolis: University of Minnesota.

KEY, V. O. (1961) Public Opinion and American Democracy. New York: Knopf.

KLAPPER, J. (1960) The Effects of Mass Communication. New York: Macmillan.

LAKOFF, S. A. (1971) "Knowledge, power, and democratic theory." Annals of the American Academy of Political and Social Science 394.

La PORTE, R. R. and D. METLAY (1975) "Technology observed: attitudes of a wary public." Science 143.

LAZARSFELD, P., B. BERELSON, and H. GAUDET (1948) The People's Choice. New York: Columbia University Press.

LEFKOWITZ, M. M., L. E. ERON, L. O. WALDER, and L. R. HUESMANN (1971) "Television violence and child agression: a follow-up study," in G. A. Comstock and E. Rubinstein (eds.) Television and Social Behavior. Washington, DC: Government Printing Office.

LIPPMANN, W. (1963) "Some notes on the press," in C. Rossiter and J. Lare (eds.) The Essential Lippmann. New York: Random House.

MACCOBY, N. and E. E. MACCOBY (1961) "Homeostatic theory in attitude change." Public Opinion Quarterly 25: 538-545.

MACHLUP, F. (1962) The Production and Distribution of Knowledge in the United States. Princeton, NJ: Princeton University Press.

McCOMBS, M. and D. SHAW (1972) "The agenda-setting function of the mass media." Public Opinion Quarterly 36: 176-187.

McDERMOTT, J. (1969) "Knowledge is power." Nation (April): 450-460.

MORRIS, R. and M. REIN (1973) "Emerging patterns in community planning," in R. Warren (ed.) Perspectives on the American Community. Skokie, IL: Rand McNally.

NIX, H. L. and N. R. SEERLEY (1973) "Comparative views and actions of community leaders and non-leaders." Rural Sociology 38.

OLIEN, C. N., G. A. DONOHUE, and P. J. TICHENOR (1968) "The community editor's power and the reporting of conflict." Journalism Quarterly 45: 243-252.

SHAW, D. L. and M. E. McCOMBS (1977) The Emergence of American Political Issues: The Agenda Setting Function of the Press. St. Paul, MN: West Publishing.

STARK, R. W. (1962) "Policy and the pros: an organizational analysis of a metropolitan newspaper." Berkeley Journal of Sociology (Spring).

STEIN, A., L. FRIEDRICH and F. VONDRACEK (1971) "Television content and young children's behavior" in G. A. Comstock and E. Rubinstein (eds.) Television and Social Behavior. Washington, DC: Government Printing Office.

VIDICH, A. J. and J. BENSMAN (1968) Small Town in Mass Society. Princeton, NJ: Princeton University Press.

WARD, J. and C. GAZIANO (1976) "A new variety of urban press: neighborhood public affairs publications." Journalism Quarterly 53: 61-67; 116.

WARREN, R. L. [ed.] (1973) Perspectives on the American Community. Skokie, IL: Rand McNally.

WERTHAM, F. C. (1952) Seduction of the Innocent. New York: Holt, Rinehart & Wonston.

5

Newspapers
and
Social Conflict

A community conflict highlights the manner in which newspapers function within the structure as instruments of information control. Actions and statements by individuals and groups take on special intensity and salience during the heat of controversy, and attention is drawn repeatedly to the newspaper's quality and quantity of reporting of the crisis.

While there may appear to be wide variation in the reporting of community controversies, editors and reporters are not independent agents in the process. Their perspectives on the situation, their range of choices, and their rationales for decisions are constrained by their roles within the community structure and by their linkages with different internal and external substructures.

Operating within a social structure does not mean that decisions are rote and predetermined from a journalist's point of view. Decisions about what to report and how to report in a highly charged, intense situation must be made more consciously and less routinely. Editors and reporters may, quite accurately, see cross-currents of the community crisis heavily influencing newspapers and other media. The tension editors and reporters experience in controversies does not result from a high degree of freedom or a wide range of alternatives; rather it indicates how restricted the choices are and how *any* course of action may have serious consequences for the newspaper as well as for the community as a whole.

When a crisis is developing within a community, editors do not have the luxury of being able to put off the decision. Often, they are not aware that a crisis is developing. A decision not to run a story is still a decision that may have ramifications for the course of the conflict and for future relationships between the newspaper and various community groups.

Newspapers are instruments for gaining public attention and, therefore, are seen as a resource by the different segments of the community seeking to gain or maintain a particular position of social and political power. Those segments include the elected officials, the governmental agencies, the business community, the churches, and citizen groups. If a conflict develops among these segments, or between these segments as a relatively unified whole and an outside agency, the newspapers may affect that conflict by reporting it and may be affected by the structure in doing so.

PHASES OF CONFLICTS

On any given day, controversies in news columns may vary widely from the new to the old. One news article may provide the first public report of a struggle between the local school board and a state agency distributing aid. Another may be a seemingly routine report which, in itself, cites no controversy, such as a story about a zoning commission's recommending a "deviance" that would allow low-income high-rise apartments in a neighborhood dominated for a century by middle-class single-family homes. Such a story may be an initial step in a developing controversy. Still another article may tell the latest chapter in a continuing dispute between the county auditor and the sheriff's department that began a year ago over use of personnel funds for purchase of patrol cars. A fourth report may center on a group of renters organizing a picket line in front of a land-lord's office, protesting a rise in rental rates, and demanding a change in services provided to renters.

Conflicts may be characterized in terms of different com-munication phases, or stages. The phases are not always sharply defined, exclusive, or in an invariable sequence, but they can be identified in many community conflicts as they develop. Con-flicts do not arise in a social vacuum. A history of related events, position alignments, and actions in a community set the stage for the development of a given controversy (Kreps and Wenger, 1973).

The *initiation* phase refers to the period when the differences at issue, or potentially at issue, are known to a small number of persons, perhaps a single individual whose knowledge of the potential conflict is a direct result of his or her position; that is, an auditor, councilman, reporter, or political party worker may learn of a situation which, if transmitted to others, is the potential focus of a community controversy. Conflict itself is a process of interaction among social roles, based upon disparities in views or positions about ends, means, or means-ends relation-ships. Although the conflict may begin as a conflict among individuals, the community nature of the conflict is revealed when it engages organized groups, agencies, or identifiable com-mon interests within the community.

The *conflict definition* phase may be simultaneous with initiation. That is, a conflict relationship may develop and become known without full clarification of the underlying issues. Conflict definition is achieved over a protracted period, as the issues are specified and articulated to groups which, if not encompassing the entire community, extend beyond the initial parties to the dispute. Conflict definition may or may not be ideological; it is ideological if it is articulated in terms of value positions which are peculiar to known interest groups. Problem definition through slogans often exemplifies an ideological per-spective.

Conflicts reach a *public* phase when the communications move into the secondary channels of the community, such as billboards, statements from speakers' platforms, court proceedings, newspaper columns, broadcast stations, or leaflets and newsletters of groups and agencies. A disparity or intense situation could conceivably be known throughout the community as a result of purely informal and private conversation and not achieve the characteristics of a community conflict. As long as a situation remains a matter of gossip, rumor, or streetcorner conversation it has not reached the public phase of controversy. Reaching that phase requires recognition of the issue by different segments of the community, generally involving such secondary communication as reporting in newspapers or broadcast channels.

There will be one or more *legitimation* phases in a conflict, when groups or certain role incumbents label the issue, or some aspect of it, as worthy in terms of basic norms and values of the community. Legitimation is not a one-time process; it may occur in many forms and through several different kinds of actions. Legitimation may be formal, as when an elected official states publicly that a protest group has "justifiable cause for concern." It may be informal, as when a group attains a certain degree of legitimacy from its demonstrated ability to muster support of large numbers of citizens in a referendum campaign. Legitimation may be qualified, as when a prestigious public figure says he or she "agrees with the concerns" of a protesting group but "not with their methods."

Questions of legitimacy often become central to a controversy. Statements by established public figures may distinguish explicitly between "the legitimate concerns of community citizens" and the "disruptive intentions" of certain protest groups. Official labeling of a group or organization as "terrorist" approaches the extreme case of defining such groupings as nonlegitimate and therefore not worthy of community attention, concern, or support. Refusal of one party in a dispute to recognize the other party as legitimate often produces conditions which some observers characterize as "rancorous" conflict (Gamson, 1966).

The initiation, conflict definition, and legitimation phases appear to be universal to most community conflicts. Other phases may be reached, depending upon the nature, extent, and organized basis for the conflict. Various diffusion phases may occur when the issues are communicated to wider groups of the public. Perhaps contending groups will announce commitments to certain courses of action and/or mobilize their resources as part of concerted action campaigns. Some conflicts dissipate shortly after initiation and problem definition; in some cases, definition or redefinition of the problem itself leads to collapse of the controversy. When the Norwalk, Connecticut, furor over blacklisting suspected subversives was redefined as a case of a local public relations campaign gone awry rather than as part of a concerted national (witch-hunting) campaign, it rapidly lost momentum and soon disappeared from all media except for a few specialized magazines that looked on the episode reflectively (Rorty, 1954; DeVoto 1954).

Some conflicts are characterized by a high degree of organization, sometimes involving new types of collective action that form specifically for the issue at hand. The disputes over power lines illustrate this point with units of farmers, landowners, and other interest groups in the affected area of construction formed in units that frequently provided symbolic acronymns, such as NPL (No Power Line); KTO (Keep Towers Out); CURE (Counties United for Rural Environment); POLE (Protect Our Land and Environment); and FACT (Families Are Concerned Too). New leaders emerge, often personifying the values and role positions of the affected group as a whole. In the case of the power-line issue in Minnesota, the new leaders tended to be middle-class and upper-middle-class farmers, lawyers, and (in at least one community) a well-known banker.

NEWSPAPERS IN CONFLICT PROCESSES

Newspapers may enter community conflicts at various points, with consequences dependent to a considerable degree on what the point of entry is and what form media attention takes. Attention by newspapers or other media may be crucial in that mass media reports may trigger or precipitate a public conflict, although basic initiation by media in the absence of other organized activity is probably infrequent. Media reports contribute to definition of the conflict by the content of articles reported and to diffusion to wider segments of the public.

Newspapers and other mass media, if they report a conflict at all, contribute to the legitimation of the conflict and/or certain points of view that are part of the conflict. In effect, *any* mention of a conflict by a newspaper has consequences for legitimation (Nnaemeka, 1976). The very recognition of a conflict confers a new status to the issue, even if the news story (or editorial) contains negative references to individuals or groups that are party to the controversy. Protest group leaders are well aware of such possibilities and frequently seek to create situations that focus media attention on the protest regardless of whether the media reporting is cast in symbols having positive or negative connotations in society at large.

Mass media often deal directly and explicitly with questions of legitimacy. Editorial positions of newspapers and broadcast stations are likely to be clear statements, either of conferral of legitimate status or withholding such status. Editorial endorsement of political candidates or positions is well-known. Editorial references to groups as "vocal minorities" may reflect withholding of legitimacy. Reference to a controversial medical treatment as a "quack cure" is one of the more extreme cases of denial of legitimacy from the community through systematic control of symbols. If military opposition to a government is labeled in the press as "guerrilla activity" or as "insurgency," that opposition has a much more legitimate character than if it is labeled as "terrorist." If today's words had been in use in 1776, the "Minutemen" of the Colonial press may well have been "terrorists" in the newspapers of London. More recently, references to the Irish Republican Army in the news media of the United Kingdom and the United States are almost without exception preceded by the term *outlawed*. Such labeling is a constant reminder about what is not considered legitimate by the established authorities of the nation and, therefore, by the major institutions of Western nations generally.

NEWSPAPER ENTRY INTO CONFLICT

While there is wide variability in conflict sequences and newspaper performance in these sequences, there are several types of newspaper entry into community conflict which recur. These "types of entry" differ in terms of when initial reporting occurs and in the form that such initial reporting takes.

One type of newspaper entry into a community controversy is described as *presentation of a local interest based upon surveillance of the external environment.* The need to keep watch over distant governmental and corporate bodies is deeply instilled in journalistic tradition and in communications institutions generally (Hocking, 1948; Rucker, 1968). Such newspaper names as Sentinel, Observer, and Guardian reflect this tradition. And while the watchdog function is not limited to the "external" environment, the focus on outside forces is particularly important in the controversies of small rural and urban communities today.

Reporting of external activity does not necessarily initiate controversy by creating the basic conditions for conflict, but it may precipitate a public phase of an issue and accelerate general attention to a new level.

One example of this type of newspaper performance is community B in southwestern Minnesota, where a small daily newspaper drew attention to a new state law establishing boundaries for regional development commissions. The newspaper editorially saw these boundaries as contrary to the interests of the local community and trade area. The newspaper went to rather unusual lengths in hiring professional economists as consultants to refute a study on which the legislated boundaries were based. The consultants' work was a principal editorial source for the newspaper's strong objections to the implications of the state law for regional development in the surrounding area. The objections were based, for example, on the reasoning that economic development regions might cross state lines rather than be confined by state boundaries as the state law provided.

A second type of newspaper entry into community controversy is a *follow-up of prior reporting in nonlocal media,* which occurs when a locally available newspaper or broadcast station oriented toward some distant and larger community is first to report a particular situation. In suburban community M, a sharp controversy was precipitated when a metropolitan area television station reported that the local city engineer had released chlorinated but otherwise raw sewage into a river from which a large urban center draws its water. The two weekly papers covering community M reported the issue the following week, emphasizing the local city engineer's point of view—runoff from melting snow had overloaded the sewage system and the urban health officer had advised him on chlorination procedures before he released the sewage.

Similarly, in community R in northwestern Minnesota, a state health agency report about toxic water in a local lake was first reported in a metropolitan newspaper with statewide circulation. The local weekly emphasized in its reports and editorials in the following weeks the potential harm of an adverse public image of its community among vacationers and sports enthusiasts.

In both communities (M and R) the newspapers came to the defense of the local community, reinforcing community identification and overlooking whatever local factional differences existed in the face of what was perceived as an attack from the outside (Vidich and Bensman, 1958). Because little basis for local conflict existed, the issue would have received little or no attention in local papers if outside media had not already reported it setting the conditions for conflict. Several observers have noted, for example, the reluctance of newspapers to do investigative reporting concerning environmental impact of local industries (Sachsman, 1976). In one case, a small daily newspaper confined its reporting of a lead industry pollution story to releases from the local company involved, even though a larger daily 150 miles away was covering the issue in considerable depth (Jensen, 1977).

There are many situations in which a specific local controversy occurs in the full glare of publicity from outside media that reach larger audiences, including the local community.

Such was the case in the Clinton, Tennessee, disturbances over racial integration of local schools in 1956, where national newspapers and broadcast stations covered the riots and National Guard units attempted to control the riots (Graham, 1967). Meanwhile, a local weekly newspaper editorially advocated acceptance of the court-ordered integration of the schools and blamed the situation on "trouble that had been brought on the community" by an anti-integration activist who had been advocating non-compliance and had organized a White Citizens Council opposition group. The activist was clearly labeled as an outsider by the newspaper: "a man who has absolutely no interest in the community, no faith in our government and no belief in the orderly processes of law."

Media techniques of organized groups may lead to reporting by outside media, stimulating local reporting beyond the usual limits of such coverage. A Minnesota weekly in a rural community in 1973 gave dramatic front-page play to the "verbal fisticuffs" of a sharp exchange between farmers and county commissioners at a county board hearing on a proposed electrical generating plant. The newspaper article indicated that television cameras (from a station in a metropolitan area 50 miles away) were at the meeting, apparently having been notified of the meeting by the protesting group of farmers.

A third type of situation in which newspapers enter into a conflict may be viewed as *primary reporting of an internal issue,* in the absence of prior reporting about the issue in external media. The newspaper's first reporting may stem from reporter activity such as routine coverage of a public meeting where a debate surfaces, from investigative efforts of reporters, from overtures from sources in agencies or interest groups, or from some combination of such actions.

City council coverage is a typical example of reporting controversy. An open exchange between a council member and a park superintendent over security measures in a city playground may precipitate a highly publicized debate over safety in city parks generally. In many communities, opposition to fluoridation of local water supplies was covered in varying ways and degrees by newspapers and other media (Crain, Katz, and Rosenthal, 1969). As indicated in previous chapters, such reporting is much more likely to occur in larger, more pluralistic communities than in small, homogeneous ones. And where it does occur, the reporting may be conducted in such a way that definitions of the conflict by established agencies and authorities dominate the news reports (Paletz, Reichert, and McIntyre, 1971).

Newspapers often receive a regular flow of press releases, letters, and other overtures from groups and individuals seeking publicity. Newspaper use of these materials, determined largely by the structural constraints within the community, may contribute to precipitation of a conflict and its subsequent development. In Norwalk, Connecticut, in 1954, a Veterans of Foreign Wars (VFW) publicity worker wrote a membership recruitment story as a press release, indicating that the local chapter was cooperating with the FBI in identifying local persons thought to be subversive. Operating in a community with a history of strong anticommunist activity, the newspaper ran the story under a banner headline, "VFW Enlists FBI Aid To Curb Subversives, Names Are Forwarded to Security Officials." This article was followed by heavy publicity in newspapers nationally, several letters to the editor of the Norwalk newspaper, a paid advertisement referring to the VFW procedures as "secret smears," and statements by the national VFW dissociating itself from such practices. At least one observer speculated later that if the recruitment story had been relegated to "the quarter column on page eight that it rated," the ensuing controversy might have been averted (Rorty, 1954). What the story "rated" was determined by the response of various community interest groups. Undoubtedly some segments of the community did regard it as "page eight material" in accord with the observer's value judgment.

NEWSPAPERS AS "ACCELERATORS" OF CONFLICT

To say that newspapers or other media *start* a controversy would be a gross oversimplification of the process. These media may, however, take part in the initiation process while playing their major role in *acceleration* of the topic to a higher and wider level of public awareness, interest, and intensity than it would have reached otherwise. Initiation and acceleration are separate processes and media may perform differently in each. Often, particularly in smaller, more homogeneous communities, the newspaper will take no part whatsoever in initiation, but will report the controversy (if at all) only after the controversy has become public through some other channel—a debate at a city council or after a formal statement of challenge by an organized group. Such a pattern has been identified in several studies of opposition to fluoridation and to nuclear power plants (Mazur, 1975).

When newspapers do participate in conflict initiation, their reporting often takes a quite different form than it will later when divisions of view have surfaced. Conflicts often develop as organized groups react to reports of events seen as bearing heavily on their collective self-interest. A report of an event might set off a confrontation without the reporters or editors necessarily anticipating such a reaction. Yet, the publication of the first announcement is crucial to the process since it gives the status of public affirmation to what was previously only informal knowledge, or possibly rumor and gossip. A public statement of a condition might come as a surprise to a community, particularly if outside agencies are involved.

The issue is not whether a topic is ignored by the press and goes relatively unnoticed, or whether it is given front-page attention and is of intense concern to the citizenry. The newspaper is a social subsystem charged with the generation and distribution of information, i.e., mass communication. The issue is: Under what conditions do newspapers play what roles in mass communication in or across communities? And what are the consequences of differential mass media attention for action by participant groups? Variation in press treatment is one salient dependent variable of the macrostructural approach, and another is the consequences for group and individual behavior to which such variation may contribute.

NEWSPAPERS AND CONFLICT: THE REGIONAL PLANNING ISSUE

The way newspapers enter community conflict is illustrated by detailed examination of two situations involving quite different topics—one in which intense conflict did not occur and one in which it did. These two situations occurred in 4 of the 19 communities of the study, 2 communities (F and K) with the political regionalization issue and 2 communities (O and S) with the power-line issue. In both situations, selected groups of news sources, editors, and reporters were interviewed shortly after the first waves of interviews with the public at large in the 4 communities. Sharp differences appear in the way the two issues were covered; the differences relate directly to the level of social organization that developed in the respective communities in connection with the issues.

During the February-May period preceding the first wave of interviews, political regionalization—or regional planning as the participants called it—was mentioned in only eight brief articles in the two communities' newspapers (Table 5-1). These articles dealt largely with organizational activity, funding problems, subregion ecology projects, and office location. When the first interviews were conducted, potential for public conflict existed between the subregion organization and the larger development commission representing the entire 11-county area in which communities F and K are located. Between May and November, the period covered by the second wave of interviews, the *Daily Times*[1] in community F carried eight articles about the subregion organization. None of the published articles was on page one; all were brief reports of rather routine events relating to funding and agency procedures. Initial expectations of heavy publicity and public controversy about organizations competing for status as regional planning centers went unfulfilled. During the interim, the subregion agency contracted with the larger commission to provide technical assistance, a factor which eliminated overlap and potential conflict. The tension in the situation was defused, and the expected controversy about regionalization did not develop.

Table 5-1 Newspaper Coverage of Political Regionalization and Power-Line Issues

	Political Regionalization			Power Line		
	Community K Weekly	Community F Daily	Community O Weekly	Community S Weekly	Regional Daily	Metropolitan Daily
Three month period before first survey						
Total items	2	6	14	8	7	3
Items on p. 1	1	0	4	3	4	0
Items on editorial page	1	–	2	1	–	–
Time of first survey	May 1-20, 1974			September 18 – October 2, 1975		
Period between first and second surveys						
Total items	2	9	11	15	12	2
Items on p. 1	1	0	5	8	5	0
Items on editorial page	–	–	2	3	1	1
Time of second survey	November 4-20, 1974			February 10-25, 1976		

ROLES OF MEDIA AND PUBLIC OFFICIALS

What was the posture of the journalists and public officials concerned with the issue? First, there *was* agreement about the importance of the topic in the abstract. The six journalists from communities F and K, and the six public officials in the county who had been active in the regional development commission, *all* agreed with the following statement, "Heavier publicity by broadcast media and newspapers would improve public understanding of regional planning." Yet, the journalists (five reporters and one weekly newspaper editor) were generally uninformed about the details of regional planning and the purposes of the two planning agencies. Five of them were unable to estimate whether leaders connected with the subregion planning agency generally agreed about regional planning, whereas the public officials had no difficulty with that question. All six of the officials were in general agreement, a good indication that at the time of the study there was little perceived conflict about the topic.

The journalists also had little information about specific proposals. Only one reporter had heard of any regional projects being proposed or planned, whereas five of the officials knew of at least one. Only one journalist had attended a regional planning meeting recently, and the journalists as a whole indicated that contacts with news sources about the topic were generally initiated by the sources, public officials. The journalists reported six different contacts about regional development, five of which were initiated by news sources. The journalists were clearly treating regional planning activities as routine news, to be received rather than sought, and not as something requiring newspaper staff initiative. Therefore, in terms of information control, most of what the public read was limited to what the agency sources provided. The situation was similar to Sachsman's (1976) finding that environmental coverage is often based largely on what agencies say. While public information services for regional planning had not yet been highly formalized, the agency was still the source of information, having the same consequences for control of information as more formalized structures. The coverage of regional planning that did occur was dependent upon agency and/or officials' overtures to the newspapers. Lack of structure possibly had the effect of keeping attention at a low level, but the passive nature of both the press and the public officials is not uncharacteristic of rural structures. Organizational activity had not developed adequately for reporters to believe that regional planning was a matter of great local concern. When asked to rank the importance of topics including regional planning, news sources picked land use and county government as most important, and reporters tended to name urban renewal, perhaps reflecting the town rather than the open-country orientation of community newspapers. While all of these topics have regional planning implications, the specific issue rather than the general and more abstract process was seen as more crucial, especially among journalists. And in the absence of specific visible issues, the journalists adopted a very passive role.

In the regional planning situation, the information control mechanisms at work resulted in a definition of the agency activity as being of relatively little concern and a situation in which reporters passively accepted information provided them by officials.

NEWSPAPERS AND CONFLICT: THE POWER-LINE ISSUE

Unlike the relatively quiescent regionalization topic, the question of location of a high-voltage power line developed into a stormy regional issue. A year after the first field interviews were conducted for this study, the issue broke into open confrontations between farm groups and power company surveyors working on the line in three different counties. Although no such confrontations had occurred when the first interviews were conducted in two communities (O and S) in the path of the proposed power line, the possibility of such clashes was a reason for selecting the issue and area as a vehicle for the study of communication and conflict. The volume of power-line cover-

age in communities along the line (O and S) may be compared
with the coverage of the regional planning issue (Table 5-1). The
coverage as reported is for the three months preceding the first
interview and does not reflect the total amount of coverage for
the period before the study. The weekly *Observer* in community O had been covering the power-line issue for nearly a year
before the first interview, and the *Sentinel* in suburban community S had covered it earlier as well. Compared with the regionalization issue, the power-line topic had clearly received more
publicity.

How and under what circumstances did the *Observer* and
Sentinel get involved in the power-line controversy? First, the
issue centered around a proposed 400-kilovolt, direct-current
power line extending from coal fields and a power plant in
North Dakota to the fringes of a metropolitan area in Minnesota. Although the specific corridor had not been established at
the time of the study, the power cooperatives preferred a
relatively straight-line route passing through seven Minnesota
counties. In its preliminary environmental reports on the proposal, the power cooperatives had indicated that about 97% of
the area traversed by the line would be agricultural land. The
stated intention was to avoid marshlands, potholes, and designated wildlife areas, as results of state environmental restrictions and farmland stability for tower construction.

Two large power cooperatives proposed the line in 1974
while seeking to negotiate with individual land owners to get
easements for construction. The proposed route at no point was
closer than about 30 miles to a community with more than
5,000 population, except near the far end where it terminated
at a substation near a metropolitan suburban area. Community
S is in that suburban area and community O is about 70 miles
to the northwest in a rural region where agriculture is the
predominant economic activity. The contacts between the
power cooperatives and landowners began in 1974. In early
1975, following strong resistance from organized farm groups
and later from local units of government, the power associations
applied to a state agency to have the power-line corridor estab-

lished in accordance with a recently enacted state power plant siting act.

The first press reports on the topic appeared in neither the *Observer* of community O nor in the *Sentinel* of suburban community S. The first press item was in the *Press* of Prairie Town (a community not in the study) 60 miles away and closer to the North Dakota state boundary. The Prairie Town *Press* carried its first article about the proposed high-voltage power line on July 4, 1974, publishing a report of a meeting between the county commissioners and representatives of the power associations. The article was a brief low-key "straight news" report. It described the general route of the line, the power association's official opinion that the lines would be minimally harmful to agriculture or homes, the height of the towers (100 to 120 feet), the cost of the line, tax payments to counties from the power associations, and the power association officials' statements of the need for additional electrical power. The article stated, without further comment or elaboration, "The bulk of the power would be used in the [metropolitan] area."

Accompanying the article was a map showing the proposed line route across the county. There was no further mention of the power line in the Prairie Town *Press* until the last half of the month (July 1974) when these items appeared:

(1) July 18: Anti-Power Line Group Sets Meeting Tonight
(2) July 25: County Group Organizes To Fight New Power Line
(3) July 25: Letter to editor from a rural citizen, urging others to write their legislators and congressmen in opposition to line
(4) August 1: Power Talks Set for Board Monday.

The last of these items carried the by-line of a local farmer with graduate training in physics and who was an officer of one of the opposition groups that held the organizational meeting a week earlier. The article was mostly about a meeting in the next county which had occurred earlier.

On August 15, the *Press* carried two long letters on the power-line issue, one from a farmer who wrote that local residents "should not and will not be reduced to compromising their standard of living either healthwise, economically, or aesthetically in order to support the reckless and unbridled energy demands of the metropolitan areas." Two weeks later, the same paper reprinted an editorial from a metropolitan daily, which foresaw new and growing conflicts arising from needs to meet energy demands. This editorial stressed the need for regional planning in siting generating plants and transmission. It also quoted a farmer (from the county served by the Prairie Town *Press*) who asked, "Why should we be forced to look at these aerial sewers just to feed air conditioners and TV sets in [metropolitan areas]?" The editorial ended, prophetically, with the note that an upcoming hearing on the issue would not be the last.

At this point, three fundamental things had happened in the development of the issue. First, active opposition had organized and achieved prominent press attention; second, the issue was clearly and repeatedly defined as a new and ominous chapter in the historical struggle between rural and urban areas; third, the rural-urban aspect of the issue was acknowledged as an issue not only locally but also by the editorial page comment of the metropolitan daily, one of the most widely circulated newspapers in the state.

On September 18, *The Daily Gazette*, a regional daily newspaper published in a city of 30,000 in the same county as community O, carried its first report on the controversy, an article about farmers with irrigated land who had met with the county commissioners to seek denial of a permit for the line.

On October 10, the weekly *Observer* in community O printed its first report on the issue, a front-page item stating that opposition was "still strong" in the area. The article itself was quite neutral and descriptive, indicating that the power associations had received a Rural Electrification Administration loan for the project, that about 15 miles of line would go through a corner of the county, that the county commissioners had yet to decide on a permit for the line, and that the line was opposed by farmers, particularly those with irrigation operations. It contained some of the same information (some in virtually verbatim form) printed in the *Daily Gazette* three weeks earlier. Both articles, for example, stated that the irrigation group was "not opposed to the power line as such" but was concerned mainly with effects on irrigated land and with consequences of corona and ozone discharges from the line.

The initial article in the *Observer* resembled the initial article in the Prairie Town *Press* three months earlier, in its neutral tone, in not mentioning specific opposition groups, and in treating the issue as tentative, with little mention of the ideological overtones. Yet the headline ("Opposition Still Strong") more than acknowledged the resistance by farmers.

In December 1974, the same metropolitan daily newspaper that had editorialized about the power-line issue in August carried a lengthy Sunday feature article, summarizing the issue and the nature of farmer resistance to the line. In April of 1975, the two power cooperatives applied to a state agency to select a corridor for the line. The state agency then scheduled a series of public hearings, following which a 20-mile-wide corridor was established.

These hearings were held in July and early August 1975, in nine different communities in areas where corridors had been proposed. They took on characteristics of adversary proceedings, with the power cooperatives and opposition groups both represented by attorneys. Technical experts, local officials, and citizens spoke or testified at different locations, with considerable cross-examination of witnesses by attorneys and much debate over certain questions: Would the lines be harmful to agriculture? Would they threaten human health? Could the lines be put underground? Questions about scientific and technical evidence came up repeatedly. In Prairie Town, where organized opposition had appeared first, a hearing was picketed by local adults and children carrying signs expressing strong opposition and open hostility to the power line. Several signs characterized the power lines as fulfilling needs of big cities at farmers' expense.

In spring and summer of 1975, the community O *Observer* devoted large amounts of space to background feature articles on technical issues concerning the line. These included the question of impact on health, especially from ozone, the effects on farming, and feasibility of underground installation which many farmer groups had favored. The paper also reported acts of opposition groups and the progress of the corridor hearing process. The nearby *Daily Gazette* concentrated on acts of agencies and opposition groups.

After the first survey in late September of 1975, coverage in the *Observer* shifted from technical arguments about the safety of the line to procedures for locating it, specific line routing, and to the opposition. A metropolitan daily editorial emphasized the need for electrical power and the *Daily Gazette* editorially stressed the need to complete the routing process. Meanwhile, the *Observer*, along with several other weeklies along the corridor route, emphasized and editorially supported the opposition.

The *Sentinel* in community S, a suburban and rural-fringe area near a metropolitan center, entered the issue even later than did the *Observer*. As late as summer of 1975, little organized opposition to the power line arose in the community S area. A single writer on the Sentinel wrote most of the paper's articles on the issue, many of which were based on information from state agency press releases or from a single source who was a member of a citizens' advisory committee. At one point in summer of 1975, the *Sentinel* reprinted an article which had earlier appeared in the *Observer*.

Apart from the editorial of August 1974 and the Sunday feature of December 1974, the metropolitan daily newspaper devoted little attention to the power-line issue; not one mention appeared in the paper from December 1974 until summer of 1975, when the paper reported the Prairie Town hearing which was picketed by local opponents of the power line. Little metropolitan television coverage of the issue occurred through 1974, 1975, and early 1976, although the topic was mentioned frequently by a regional television station located in a small rural community near the middle of the proposed power-line corridor.

REPORTERS, SOURCES, AND THE POWER LINE

One of the characteristics of the languishing regional planning topic was apparent journalistic passivity; reporters said the news sources had initiated five of their six contacts on the issue. Furthermore, the reporters were relatively uninformed about possible actions that might be taken under regional planning.

In the power-line situation, reporter involvement was much greater. Six reporters, including two from daily newspapers, and 14 sources were interviewed in the fall of 1976, after the power-line corridor was established but before a specific route was selected. Five of these reporters agreed that the power-line issue was "very important." When asked about the 10 specific news articles written on the topic, the reporters indicated that 8 articles had either been their own idea or suggestions from other journalists, such as the editor of the particular newspaper. In only 2 cases did these reporters specify that the story had been suggested by a source; one was the same source that supplied most copy on the power-line issue at the time for the *Sentinel* of community S, and the other was a source in a power association. Sources confirmed that reporters made most initial contacts on these articles, contrasting sharply with the regional planning topic, in which sources initiated a majority of contacts.

In addition, the reporters covering the power line were getting information and views from various sides of the issue. When asked to name their different sources, the six reporters identified 26 different persons, groups, or documents: 7 were anti-power-line sources, 9 were pro-power-line sources, and 10 were either scientists and technicians not directly involved, politicians, or members of state environmental agencies.

Did the sources see these newspaper reports as having any impact on the course of the controversy? Two questions on this point were asked of the 14 sources (Table 5-2). One was whether the local media (including newspapers) made a difference to the individual "in making up your mind about the power line corridor issue." Of the 14 sources, 4 said yes, and they

Table 5-2 Sources' Views of Media Impact on Power-Line Issue

	Yes	No	Total
Question:			
Have the local newspapers, radio stations made a difference to you, in making up your mind about the power line corridor issue?	4	10	14
As far as you can recall, did the article, or information in the (specific) article, affect any decision that your organization or agency was making at the time?	4	10	14

explained that media "made a difference" largely in terms of increasing the ability of their organizations to take newly publicized issues and points of view into account. As one source said: "It [media coverage] probably affects the way we approach the problem but not the decision. If there is a lot of public opinion on this issue in the paper, we tend to react by the way we approach our community awareness activities." Another said, "If there are issues that have been reported that we never considered earlier, then we bring [these issues] into focus.

Of the four seeing such impact, three said the newspapers were the most important of the media in "making a difference." The other source mentioned television.

Among the nine sources who said the media had made "no difference" to them in making up their minds, the most common reason was superior and prior information which the source claimed to have, usually because of organization, profession, or position. One technical expert put it this way: "Well, I may be a little different from other people because I am an engineer. The things that radio, TV and newspapers would say wouldn't affect me because I wouldn't take what they say as gospel truth as most people would. I would do my own research and dig into the issue myself." This expert's view is typical, in the sense that it includes the belief that media affect people in general but not the individual who has specialized expertise. A farm organization leader said: "Basically, we are giving them information rather than they giving us information. With at least 90% of the articles, I know what's going to be in it before it is published.

The latter comment was largely supported by the source group as a whole. When asked directly in a second question whether a specific article contained "any information that was new to you or to any agency or organization with which you are associated," only 1 of the 14 sources said yes. Responses indicate that whatever technical information there is to be dispensed already resides with the agencies and organizations which these sources represent. They apparently viewed the media reports more in terms of what they indicated about public reaction than what they contained in terms of technical facts. Four sources referred, bluntly, to what they saw as the newspapers' inability to understand the problem or to get facts straight.[2]

A second question was whether any particular news article had affected any decision that the source's organization or agency was making at the time. Of the 14 sources, 4 cited such effects, largely of the kind mentioned in answer to the first question. Reporters were also asked whether, as far as they knew, the specific news articles they wrote affected decisions that "some organization or agency was making at the time." Only one reporter answered yes, saying: "It affected the scope of the [anti-power-line] organization. As more farmers became interested, they either joined the group or offered support." In general, neither sources nor reporters had high estimates of newspaper impact on the *organizations and agencies* in the dispute. This finding is consistent with the conclusion that the newspapers were disseminating information, about facts and events generated within these organizations, to a wider public. They took part in widening the scope of the conflict, but initiation began with the organization of opposition groups. Newspapers were directly instrumental at the initiation stage largely through reporting specific events and occurrences. Their reporting of issues did not occur until after opposition groups were established and visible.

NEWSPAPERS AND ORGANIZED SOCIAL ACTION

Merton and Lazarsfeld (1948) emphasized the importance of publicity in *initiating* action, particularly when that action is an enforcement of social norms. Corruption in politics may be generally known, they said, but no organized action occurs until there is a public *announcement* portraying that corruption as a clear deviation from social norms.

To the extent that the two cases reviewed here are typical of community conflicts, the conception of media as *initiating* social action appears to require considerable refinement. The above examination of the two situations—one in which a potential controversy did not develop and one where it did—emphasizes the primacy of social organization itself in the development of a conflict. Newspapers and other media neither cause that organization nor stand apart from it. The media are part of a process out of which new organizations may form and mobilize. As has been stressed throughout this analysis, they function as mechanisms of information control which are alternately distributive and feedback. That publicity and media play a role is evident, but the *specific* role or roles in initiation, perpetuation, or closure need greater clarification.

At the outset, in both the regional planning and the power-line issues, newspapers performed in terms of distribution control, with reporting centering largely around *events*. Distribution control occurs within the social system at points where information about key events may be received and is capable of being transmitted to the larger audience. The reports of the regional development agencies and the early reports about the power-line issue were similar in that, in both cases, the reports had a routine character. Even in the power-line episode, the first article about the power-line proposal in the Prairie Town *Press* did not mention opposition as such. The article was a descriptive report, that is, control of information through distribution. Most of the reports on other topics, in the same edition, had the same character.

In every newspaper examined, first reports of the controversial nature of the issue appeared after some form of organized

opposition appeared. At that point, reporting and other communications occurred which had a feedback control quality; the
information dealt specifically with sharp differences in views
and actions. The Prairie Town *Press,* after the initial report,
contained several letters to the editor on the power line. A rural
woman wrote a letter urging opposition and stating certain
technical characteristics of the line; a power cooperative public
relations official later wrote a letter taking issue with the
woman's version of the facts; an opposition group leader still
later wrote a letter to the editor challenging the public relations
official's version of the line's effects.

Letters to the editor often reflect organized activity directly,
with important consequences as a result. A letter may alert an
editor to the possibility of a future issue in the community, but
the isolated individual letter is also easily dismissed as the work
of a crank. Formation of a protest group with a name, however,
bears a degree of credibility and legitimacy that only a few
high-status individuals acting independently could attain.
Whether the new organization is a protest group or an advocacy
group, it has potential consequences for participation and involvement that do not necessarily exist with established agencies.

In the case of the regional planning commission, a matrix of
organizational linkages had not developed. An important principle of organization is emphasis upon in*ter*- as well as in*tra*organization. One of the bases of social power and control is the
way in which a group relates to the organizational matrix as a
whole.

As a fledgling bureaucracy, the regional planning commission
had little citizen participation. Its membership was specified by
statute (mayors, county board members, representatives of
other units of government), and its contact with voluntary
groups at the time of the study was extremely limited. In the
case of the power line, the report of plans to construct a line
through a region may have been a reinforcing event in stimulating the organization of one of the first opposition groups.
Many landowners had already been contacted individually on
the question of easements for the power line; the first reports in

the newspaper in that period defined the question as a regional concern.

Once the organizations were formed, the community newspaper coverage took on a tone of strong opposition to the line, and the feedback control aspects of this reporting became narrowly defined. The *Observer,* the *Sentinel,* and the other weekly newspapers in the area such as the Prairie Town *Press* generally emphasized local opposition to the exclusion of whatever local disagreement there may have been on the point. Their performance in this regard was highly predictable in terms of community structure. In a period of dramatic social encounter, the community newspaper may act as a mechanism for social maintenance and portray the community as unified against an "outside intruder" even if there is considerable evidence that sharp divisions exist within the community as to whether the event at issue is an intrusion or a benefit to the local good.

In fact, different views were expressed on the power-line question within these rural communities. In every county, there were electric cooperative association directors, often influential citizens who had been active over a 30-year period or longer in bringing electrical power to the countryside. To such groups of leaders who identified with the farmer cooperative ideology of the pre- and post-World War II years—and with the REA generally—opposition by farmers to power lines being proposed by *cooperatives* bordered on being an act of sacrilege.[3] But except for an occasional letter to an editor from one of these directors, the traditional cooperative ideology was largely ignored in the local papers. Many of the letter writers and some of the community newspaper writers themselves referred to the power associations as "power companies."

A point may come in the development of a controversy when initiative passes from organizations and/or agencies to the media. At this point media personnel define the issue as "news" and therefore a topic which they will follow up regularly and energetically. This point appears to be reached when media roles define the issue as one of community-wide concern. When that happens, sources can expect to be called or contacted by the newspapers and other media. They need no longer initiate all of the contacts themselves, although there will often continue to be competition among sources for press space.

When a controversy reaches this news definition stage, the newspapers' role in the process may undergo some change. New events related to the issue are reported immediately and with prominent display. The newspapers take editorial positions and become generally identified with a point of view. In community O, for example, the editor of the *Observer* was also a chamber of commerce officer and, at one public hearing on the power-line issue, read a statement of the chamber expressing strong opposition to the line. The statement put the community's organized leadership on record with a point of view, thus creating an image of community solidarity with the affected farmers. In fact, as subsequent surveys in that community were to indicate, pronounced differences in opinions existed there.

The particular involvement of the *Observer* editor, as a spokesman for a local leadership group, may or may not be unusual. However, the newspaper as an instrument of information control serving a community solidarity function often accomplishes the same result even if the editor is less visible in the local leadership structure. That is, visibility may not be as important as editor identification with that leadership structure. Two earlier studies suggest that if editors identify with the community leadership or are identified with it by others (Edelstein and Schulz, 1963; Olien, Tichenor, and Donohue, 1968), they are more likely to perform in terms of maintaining community consensus. Evidence from the power-line controversy is consistent with that finding. In three other communities (other than O and S), community newspapers gave prominent attention to the opposition and, when they editorialized, supported the anti-power-line groups.

Newspapers in a controversy with a common regional cause may present a common regional front. In the power-line area, community papers occasionally reprinted each other's editorials and, in some cases, news and feature articles on the topic. In one case, a community newspaper reprinted an editorial from a college newspaper which had been critical of the power-line proposal.

Such mutual support and sharing of comment and reports among community newspapers does not mean that all newspapers will have the same reporting *or* editorial policy on the issue. Differences are often quite predictable according to the information control functions of media in communities of different types. During the study period, two daily newspapers covered the power-line topic in some detail and commented on it editorially. One is the metropolitan newspaper (with circulation of more than 200,000) and the other is the regional *Daily Gazette* in the same county as community O. In both cases, the daily papers' news reports concentrated on the controversy itself, particularly events and statements of the opposing groups, with relatively little attention to technical aspects of the issue. Also, and more important in terms of social maintenance, these newspapers editorially treated the farmers' concerns as worthy of consideration but insufficient to halt the construction of the line. The regional daily referred specifically to a "minority" of farmers opposed to the line, emphasizing instead the need for electrical power. These editorial positions of the dailies spoke to the concerns of urban communities, in effect reinforcing the small town and rural viewpoint that rights of individuals and prerogatives of local communities take second place to concerns of urban centers. In such a situation, the traditional rural-urban conflict is acerbated by editorializing which may be functional for the maintenance of the urban communities whose value structure the dailies primarily address, reflect, and reinforce.

SUMMARY

Conflict is a principal ingredient of social change. Mass media such as newspapers contribute to this process without necessarily being advocates of change per se. The conflicts have their roots in social differentiation, and newspapers contribute to the increasing intensity and widening scope of these conflicts while performing in their traditional roles. Examination of such episodes provides further support to Glenn's (1974) conclusion that mass media are not reducing the difference in attitudes and orientations between rural and urban sectors of society.

Newspapers, or mass media generally, function as a necessary component of a system's institutional technology for dealing with conflict, a major process associated with social change and adaptation. Media constitute a part which is necessary, but not sufficient in and of itself or causal in the conflict process.

NOTES

1. Newspaper names throughout the book are pseudonyms.

2. While the news sources cited various specific inaccuracies in about half of the articles, all except two of the articles were judged by the sources to be "generally accurate." The specific inaccuracies cited frequently had to do with incorrect names (or titles) and with incorrect numerical data. For example, a power association official noted that the cooperative was referred to in an article as a "company" and not as an "association." Other inaccuracies cited concerned the voltage of the line, the number of acres potentially affected, numbers of persons attending and/or testifying at hearings, and the question of whether the governor had any authority in the routing or the power-line corridor. In only two cases did sources regard the reporters as "incapable," and not a single source indicated unwillingness to work with the same reporter in the future.

3. REA refers to Rural Electrification Administration, a unit of the U.S. Department of Agriculture formed in the New Deal era to provide loans to regional and local cooperative electric associations. The letters *REA* are so widely used that local electric cooperatives in rural areas are traditionally referred to by citizens as "The REA." The fact that the power associations involved in the high-voltage power-line issue were not given the "REA" label either in the press or in local parlance symbolizes a sharp redefinition of the large electric power cooperatives. This symbolic redefinition occurred in spite of the fact that the first article in the community O *Observer* reported an REA loan to the power associations for the power-line project. The fact that the power associations developing the transmission line proposal are not directly in charge of local distribution of power may have contributed to the fact that citizens did not use the REA label in referring to the associations.

REFERENCES

BERNARD, J. (1962) American Community Behavior. New York: Holt, Rinehart & Winston.
COLEMAN, J. S. (1957) Community Conflict. New York: Macmillan.

CRAIN, R. L., E. KATZ, and D. B. ROSENTHAL (1969) The Politics of Community Conflict: The Fluoridation Decision. Indianapolis, IN: Bobbs-Merrill.

DeVOTO, B. (1954) "Norwalk and points west." Harpers Magazine (April).

EDELSTEIN, A. and J. B. SCHULZ (1963) "The leadership role of the weekly newspaper as seen by community leaders: a sociological perspective" pp. 221-238 in L. A Dexter and D. M. White (eds.) People, Society and Mass Communication. New York: Macmillan.

GAMSON, W. (1966) "Rancorous conflict in community politics." American Journal of Sociology 31.

GLENN, N. D. (1974) "Recent trends in intercategory differences in attitudes." Social Forces 52: 395-401.

GRAHAM, H. D. (1967) Crisis in Print: Desegregation and the Press in Tennessee. Nashville: Vanderbilt University Press.

HOCKING, W. (1948) Freedom of the Press. Chicago: University of Chicago Press.

JENSEN, D. (1977) "The loneliness of the environmental reporter." Columbia Journalism Review (February).

KREPS, G. and D. E. WENGER (1973) "Toward a theory of community conflict: factors influencing the initiation and scope of conflict." Sociological Quarterly 14.

MAZUR, A. (1975) "Opposition to technological innovations." Minerva 13 (spring): 58-81.

MERTON, R. and P. LAZARSFELD (1948) "Mass communication, popular taste and organized social action," pp. 492-512 in W. Schramm (ed.) Mass Communications. Urbana: University of Illinois Press.

NNAEMEKA, T. I. (1976) "Issue legitimation, mass media functions and public knowledge of social issues." Ph.D. dissertation, University of Minnesota.

OLIEN, C. N., G. A. DONOHUE, and P. J. TICHENOR (1968) "The community editor's power and the reporting of conflict." Journalism Quarterly 45 (summer): 243-252.

PALETZ, D. L., P. REICHERT, and B. McINTYRE (1971) "How the media support local governmental authority." Public Opinion Quarterly 35.

RORTY, J. (1954) "Thirty days that shook Norwalk." Commentary Magazine (April).

RUCKER, B. (1968) The First Fredom. Carbondale: Southern Illinois University Press.

SACHSMAN, D. B. (1976) "Public relations influence on coverage of environment in the San Francisco area." Journalism Quarterly 53.

VIDICH, A. J. and J. BENSMAN (1958) Small Town in Mass Society. Princeton, NJ: Princeton University Press.

6

Community Conflict
and
Citizen Knowledge

Whenever there is a community-wide debate, whether it is about a nuclear power plant, an urban renewal project, or location of a chemical waste disposal site, the question arises about whose ox is being gored. Such events usually produce social conflict, which results in groups considering their interests as being sacrificed for the greater good. They then struggle to redefine priorities in society at large. The issue, as Lippmann (1922) pointed out, creates the relevant publics. When a nuclear power plant is proposed as a way of solving society-wide energy needs, groups form to participate in the decision to accept or reject the proposed solution or redefinition of the problem. Many argue that an even greater societal interest lies in protecting individual rights and local control over the community or region's future. The style of life implied in the local autonomy perspective includes these interests as well as needs for energy or possible alterations of lifestyle resulting from lack of sufficient energy.

If a group lacks numbers, it must organize as a minority and use effective techniques to get its case before the public. The group must anticipate that speaking out with a collective voice will trigger answers from the established agencies proposing the facility. This sets the stage for a possible conflict situation. Information such as scientific evidence about nuclear fallout and its effects on health becomes important not because of abstract concern about public understanding, but because information is vital resource in the struggle for public support. Armed with whatever information and expertise they can marshal, groups seek to enlist the attention and/or open support of mass media in waging the struggle.

These debates raise important questions about the consequences of conflict and conflict strategies. Among them is the question about the consequences of heated controversy for citizen knowledge, for example, the cherished belief that communication does not lead to greater understanding between source and audience in a conflict situation. Long-standing statements appear in academic literature (Lundberg, 1939; Bogardus, 1920) that conflict inevitably leads to "communication breakdowns" and to general confusion. Whenever a public disagreement about interpretation of scientific evidence occurs as in, say, the question about banning cyclamates, specialists in relevant research disciplines frequently decry the "misinformation" on the issue. According to these views, conflict arouses high levels of emotion, leading people neither to communicate rationally nor to understand well what others may have said. Selective distortion, both in sending and receiving messages, is thought to increase in proportion to the intensity of the conflict. Such reasoning is akin to the view in some social science literature that conflict is a symptom of social disorganization and pathological deviancy. Although the disorganization perspective has been challenged (e.g., Feagin, 1974), social programs often cite some version of it as a basis for confining participation in public decision making to a minimal number of groups, therefore limiting the potential for controversy. This perspective may have limited validity as regards general social stability, but is a rationale for maintenance of the power elite as primary decision makers.

Data from several phases of the Minnesota community research program provide a basis for testing the hypothesis that the higher the level of perceived conflict about an issue in a community, the higher the level of knowledge about that issue. This hypothesis assumes that conflict is a regular, predictable outcome of organization among countervailing groups participating in social action and that conflict is a stimulator of communication and interest in the issue. So as conflict and communication rise, there should be a resultant increase in familiarity with the issue in question and with knowledge about various facets of the issue.

This "conflict-knowledge" hypothesis is based upon a variety of considerations associated with the conflict theory school of thought. Several scholars in this tradition have referred to the role of conflict in arousing and maintaining citizen involvement (Coser, 1956; Dahrendorf, 1959). Conflict in this perspective is a basic social process that stimulates a wide range of communicative and other activity.

One kind of stimulation from conflict, in a social system, is a revitalization of old norms (Coser, 1967). Community struggles over language, sexual references, and other cultural and religious symbols in text books frequently draw renewed attention to such fundamental norms as family solidarity, the work ethic, and community identity. Confrontations between segregationists and school boards over racial mixing of school populations often gave new focus to traditional values such as maintaining social order and "observing the law of the land" (Graham, 1967). Clashes over so-called antisubversive activity in several U.S. communities during the decade immediately following World War II often led to renewed attention to basic notions of fair play and due process in the American system.

A second kind of stimulation possible from conflict, according to Coser, can lead to a redefinition of old norms or emergence of new ones. Labor conflict between teachers and school boards may produce a redefinition of the rights of public employees and of the negotiation process in a given community. When urban-trained educators actively and publicly justified avantgarde reading materials, the textbook controversies cited above may have drawn increased attention to alternative lifestyles and norms of personal conduct. Also, conflict over employment practices, such as that generated by affirmative action regulations and statutes, has to some extent led to a redefinition of the process of filling a wide range of occupational positions.

Third, conflict theorists frequently point to the consequences for building and strengthening internal cohesion, within a group or larger community. A town struggling to keep its main industry alive despite strong federal and state environmental agency pressure to close it may witness a growing "we-feeling" as citizens band together to achieve a common purpose. Recent concern over outside land speculation in at least one Canadian community led to a previously unlikely coalition between Hutterite and non-Hutterite farmers, in the form of a joint petition for protectionist provincial laws (Obeng-Quaidoo, 1977). As recently as 20 years ago, the same two groups had been locked in often bitter disputes over the Hutterites' land-owning and communal farming practices.

THE CONFLICT-KNOWLEDGE HYPOTHESIS

According to a conflict theory perspective, then, conflict may be seen as a necessary process but not a sufficient condition for maximum diffusion of information about social problems. If conflict leads to renewed emphasis on traditional norms, emergence of new ones, or to new levels of social cohesion, a change or increase in communication is implied. Such communication may occur at primary levels or at secondary levels including newspapers and other mass media channels.

Communication and conflict intensity are often related in a reciprocal way. Dissemination of information by a newspaper or other mass medium can quickly lead to acceleration of an issue through creation of widespread awareness of a potential or acknowledged conflict situation. And, as pointed out illustratively in Chapter 5, the existence of an organized basis for conflict often produces new and accumulative forms of communication through a variety of channels, including both primary and secondary contracts. The diffusion literature (North Central Region Publication, 1955; Rogers, 1962; Katz, 1955; Coleman, Menzel, and Katz, 1966) would lead to the expectation that the primary, interpersonal communication stimulated by conflict intensity would be a principal mechanism in producing higher levels of information.

The conflict-knowledge hypothesis, then, is that the higher the level of perceived conflict about an issue in a community, the higher the level of knowledge about that issue. This hypothesis assumes reciprocal links among mass media coverage, perception of conflict, and primary communication, with conflict as the basic factor. As conflict and communication rise, an increase in familiarity with the issue in question and with knowledge about various facets of the issue should result.

MEASURES USED TO TEST THE
CONFLICT-KNOWLEDGE ANALYSIS

In addition to the measures of knowledge and familiarity described in Chapter 2, the analysis involved a measure of media coverage. Community mass media coverage for each issue was estimated according to content in locally circulated newspapers. This estimate, called the newspaper coverage index, is a weighted total of all articles about a topic appearing in newspapers that circulate in the community during the six-month period preceding the survey. The number of articles about an issue in a given newspaper was multiplied by the proportion of persons in the sample who reported reading the newspaper in which those articles appeared. Values on the index ranged from a low of zero for the mercury issue in community Q to a high of 57.29 for an environmental issue in community J.

FINDINGS AND THE CONFLICT-KNOWLEDGE HYPOTHESIS

One part of the conflict-knowledge hypothesis is the expectation that higher levels of publicity are correlated with a greater

degree of perceived conflict about an issue. Data are supportive
of that expectation (rank correlation = .58, p < .01), although
the array of issues in the scatter diagram suggests that the
differences are by type of issue as well as by amount of
coverage (Figure 6-1), a finding which supports the interactive

Figure 6.1   Newspaper Coverage Index and Perceived
Conflict for 27 Community Issue Comparisons

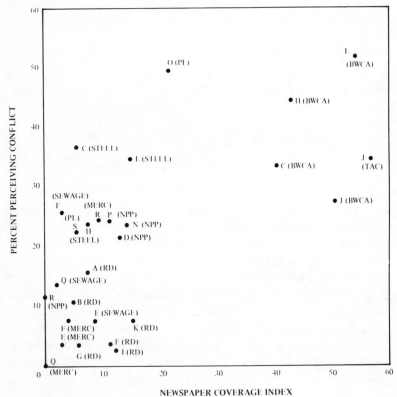

Key:

BWCA = Mining in Boundary
    Waters Canoe Area issue

tac = Taconite issue

RD = Regional Development
    issue

NPP = Nuclear power plant
    issue

Merc = Mercury pollution
    issue

sewage = Sewage control
    issue

PL = Power line issue

steel = Steel plant issue

aspects of the hypothesis. The cases in the upper-right corner of the scatter are very similar issues. All had received heavy state-wide coverage and all involved differences between environmentalist groups, largely from metropolitan areas, and local groups. These environmental issues developed in the late 1960s and early 1970s, when ecology was a highly popular topic and tensions between environmental concerns and local prerogatives were first becoming apparent. Four of these cases, for example, concern the question of whether mining should be permitted in or near a large wilderness area, most of which was reserved for nonmotorized recreational use.

A second aspect of the conflict-knowledge hypothesis is that the higher the perceived conflict about an issue, the more interpersonal communication about that issue within the community. This expectation is based upon the stimulation that conflict produces for everyday life and conversation. Once definition of a conflict is developed, it becomes a part of the agenda for interpersonal discourse. Conflict is cumulative in nature, continuing until an accommodation among the conflicting groups is reached.

Data on perception of conflict (an open-end measure) support this part of the hypothesis. The rank correlation across community issues between community levels of perception of conflict and community levels of discussion is .50 ($p < .01$). The scattergram for the relationship is in Figure 6-2.

A next question is whether interpersonal communication is linked to knowledge, and data support the hypothesis that the two are related (Figure 6-3). For the 24 comparisons for which relevant measures are available, the rank difference correlation between amount of interpersonal communication and familiarity with the issue is .84 ($p < .01$). The relationship is strong and fairly straightforward, quite in line with a diffusion model, in that primary conversation tends to widen topic familiarity. Again, issues cluster somewhat, with regional development topics in the lower-left part of the scatter diagram. Even within that topical area, however, there is a tendency for higher levels of discussion to be associated with higher familiarity.

Figure 6.2   Perception of Conflict in the Issue and
Interpersonal Communication for 24 Community
Issue Comparisons

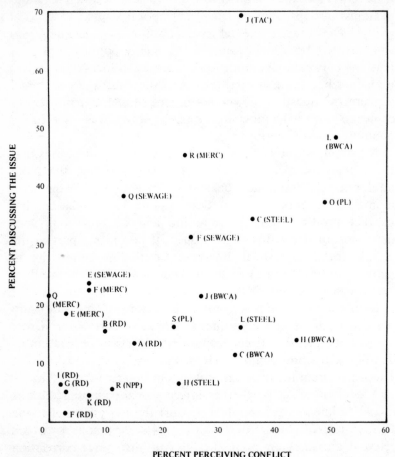

A direct relationship exists between perception of conflict
and familiarity (Figure 6-4). Again, the higher the conflict, the
higher the familiarity, although the relationship is not as strong
as between interpersonal communication and familiarity (.51,
p < .01, versus .84).

While these data do not lend themselves to a multiple regres-
sion analysis, the pattern of rank correlations is consistent with

Figure 6.3   Percent Discussing the Issue and Percent
Familiar with the Issue in 24 Community Issue Comparisons

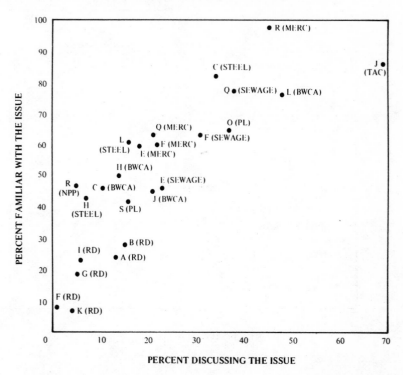

the view that newspaper coverage is correlated with high levels
of conflict which in turn is associated with higher levels of
awareness. The rank-order correlation coefficients, when
arranged as in Table 6-1, tend to increase from left to right,
with the stronger links between conflict and interpersonal communication and between interpersonal communication and
familiarity. Newspaper coverage is linked to development of
conflict but is only weakly linked (.09) to familiarity. These
results suggest that when data across communities are examined
on topics such as these, the effect of newspaper publicity on
increasing awareness and familiarity with an issue is largely
indirect. It is general level of conflict, in which newspapers play
a reciprocal role, that appears basic to stimulating citizens to
learn about an issue.

Figure 6.4   Percent Perceiving Conflict and Percent
Familiar with the Issue in 27 Community Issue Comparisons

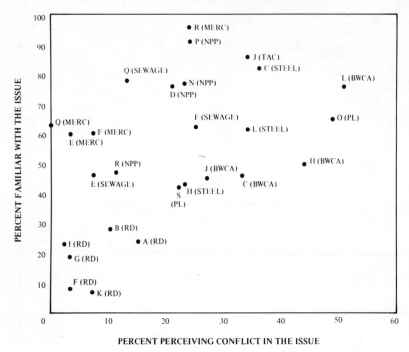

CONFLICT AND KNOWLEDGE: A PAIR OF CASE STUDIES

More detailed examination of the regionalization and power-line cases offered greater insight into the processes and relationships among conflict, dissemination of information, and citizen knowledge. These controversies, as described in Chapters 1 and 5, provided an opportunity for studying these processes over time. Each case involves measures at different points in time during a period when increasing numbers of groups and agencies were being drawn into one controversy (the power line) while activity and attendant publicity was slackening in the other (regional planning).

Both communities in the regional planning study are in the same county of an 11-county region. Community K, with

Table 6-1   Rank Correlations Among Communication Factors,
Conflict and Knowledge, Across Community Issue Comparisons

	1 Newspaper Coverage Index	2 Perception of Conflict	3 Interpersonal Communication	4 Familiarity With Issue
1. Newspaper Coverage Index	X			
2. Perception of Conflict	.58	X		
3. Interpersonal Communication	.08	.50	X	
4. Familiarity with Issue	.09	.51	.84	X

population under 2,000, was once a farm service center, but is now partly a bedroom community for commuting workers. Nearby townships are dominated largely by farming, and the entire area is served by a weekly paper, the *Chronicle.* The other community, F, population near 30,000, is a transportation and small-scale manufacturing center with a number of ethnic groups, four-year colleges, and more than 1,000 places of business. The daily *Forum* serves the community which, compared with many cities of its size, has a decidedly urban atmosphere.

As indicated earlier, the anticipated heavy publicity focusing on competing organizations and public controversy about regional planning did not develop in either the *Chronicle* or the *Forum* between the first and second interviews.

The power-line study also involved two areas, described in Chapter 5. One is in a rural county near and including Community O, population under 2,500, an agricultural trade and service center with relatively few residents commuting to other cities for work. The weekly *Observer* circulates locally and in surrounding farm areas. The community O area also includes several rural townships northwest of the town and other townships to the east. All rural townships are largely agricultural and relatively homogeneous in ethnic background.

Community S, the other study area in the power-line issue, includes two adjacent incorporated places. They are Metville, with a population of about 6,000, and Metfield, with 3,000 persons living mostly on farms and former farmsteads. Community S as a whole has more total population, a higher concentration of young people, more places of business, and a wider variety of professions and occupations than community O. Both Metville and Metfield are served by two jointly owned weekly papers which are different regional editions of the same basic newspaper. Since they carried identical coverage of the power-line topic, both are referred to as the *Sentinel*.

Among the different power-line study areas, the controversy varied in intensity even at the time of the first interviews. In the community O area, especially strong opposition arose in townships northwest of town, where power association representatives and landowners discussed easements before the power associations asked the state agency to designate a corridor. However, few talked seriously about the line going through the incorporated limits of community O itself or through the townships to the east.

In the community S area, concerns were quite different, focusing on residential areas and the hearing procedure itself, in part because end points of the line had been fixed before the corridor hearings began. At a major corridor hearing there in August 1975, statements emphasized that regardless of other corridor routes, the lines would go through both Metville and Metfield, near the end of the line.

In mid-September 1975, a citizens' advisory committee recommended to the state agency that the corridor be diverted from most of the agricultural area northwest of community O where the proposed line had been hotly disputed. On October 3, 1975, the state agency designated a corridor that accepted most of the area proposed by the hearing officer, including much of the area sharply opposed by farmers and suburban residents. As a result, the agency designation was not in agreement with several recommendations of the advisory committee.

The first interviews in the power-line study were conducted

between September 18 and October 2, 1975, just before the corridor designation. A short time later, the power associations applied to another state agency for a certificate of need, emphasizing a projected increase in demand for electrical power by their rural consumer members. The certificate of need had not yet been issued when the second wave of interviews was conducted between February 10 and the end of February 1976. Hearings, however, had been held, both on the certificate of need and on specific routes for the line. In late January 1976, the state agency specified certain routes that the power line could take within the larger corridor areas, routes similar to those proposed by the power associations. Those routes went through the rural townships northwest of community O and crossed both sections of community S.

MEDIA COVERAGE

Compared with regional planning, the power-line question received considerable publicity in weekly newspapers serving both study areas. Whereas regional planning publicity centered around routine reports, the power-line coverage included articles about the intense opposition to the line, to procedures, and to interpretations of scientific evidence about effects of the line. Before the first interviews, the community O *Observer* devoted large amounts of space to technical issues. After the first interviews, coverage particularly in the *Observer* shifted from technical arguments about the safety of the line to procedures for locating it, specific line routing, and to opposition.

At the time of the interviews, regional development and the power-line issue represented sharp contrasts in social organization, events, and media coverage. Regional planning was largely at the initiating stage and received low-key treatment by newspapers. The power-line topic, however, already had dimensions of an intense issue within the respective regions. Opposition groups had formed, first to deal with technical issues and later with procedure and organized protest and legal counteraction.

WHAT PEOPLE KNOW ABOUT PUBLIC ISSUES

The varying levels of media attention to the issues are reflected in the differing levels of familiarity and understanding which respondents expressed on regional planning and the power-line issue. In the first and second interviews on regionalism, no more than 8% had any accurate knowledge about the purpose of the regional development commissions and no more than 5% knew how the commissions were funded (Table 6-2). Though these levels are low, they tended to decline even more in the second interviews—not a single respondent in community K knew the commission's purpose. The highest specific knowledge on the topic was on the subregion organization, which had been part of the structure for a longer period of time; 12% in community K had some accurate knowledge about it in the first study. Familiarity dropped sharply (to 3%) in the second interview, after the subregion agency had been absorbed quietly into the larger one, in what might be considered an accommodation to avoid an increase in conflict.

Between a fourth and a third of the respondents had some accurate information on "revenue sharing," which is a concept related to regional planning.

In spite of the lack of knowledge about specifics, at least a fifth of the citizens saw the regional planning issue as "very important" and a third or more said "yes" when asked if it were a "touchy subject."

The power-line issue was characterized by higher levels of general familiarity, higher rated importance, and higher levels of perceived conflict in the rural and open country areas than the regional planning issue. The proportion of citizens having some accurate knowledge about the power line varied from a low of 25% in the suburban community to a high of 70% or more in the most directly affected northwest rural area (Table 6-3).

However, even with the continuing heavy publicity, overall levels of measured knowledge on the power-line topic did not increase between the first and second interviews. On specific

Table 6-2 Specific Items of Knowledge About Regional
Planning

	Community K		Community F	
	1st	2nd	1st	2nd
Percent who:	(N:194)	(N:183)	(N:187)	(N:92)
Have any accurate knowledge about "RDC" purpose.	8%	0%	7%	2%
Know how "RDC" is funded.	4%	2%	5%	3%
Have *any* accurate information on "revenue sharing."	28%	23%	33%	28%
Have *any* accurate knowledge about "sub-region organization" purpose.	12%	3%	3%	2%
Rate issue as "very important."	22%	29%	20%	20%
Call topic a "touchy subject."	33%	39%	36%	33%

aspects, some changes occurred with slight increases in percent
hearing about effects on health in all except the suburban
community (Table 6-4). On other aspects, including effects on
agriculture, underground installation, names of utilities, and
names of organizations opposed, declines equaled increases in
familiarity.

This last finding may suggest a modification of the conflict-
knowledge hypothesis. While conflict increases awareness of a
topic, it may not necessarily lead to increased understanding of
the underlying issues in the population at large. Perhaps as the
issue progresses, newspaper coverage shifts to some extent from
concentration on the scientific and technical aspects to concentration on procedure and legal opposition. The conflict itself, as
a conflict, becomes the story. Accordingly, the percent calling
the topic a "touchy subject" increased in four of the five study
areas, particularly in the rural townships most directly affected.
In this situation, however, one might not expect appreciable
changes of knowledge about specific technical aspects of the
issue.

Table 6-3 Knowledge and Opinions About the Power-Line Issue in two studies*

Knowledge and Familiarity	Community S			
	Metville		Metfield	
	(N:68)	(N:48)	(N:39)	(N:43)
Percent who:	1st	2nd	1st	2nd
Have any accurate knowledge about the power line.	33%	25%	49%	49%
Say issue is "very important."	18%	21%	22%	46%
Say issue "affects me directly."	31%	25%	22%	44%

	Community O					
	Town		Rural area, East		Rural area, Northwest	
	(N:71)	(N:48)	(N:34)	(N:33)	(N:31)	(N:36)
Percent who:	1st	2nd	1st	2nd	1st	2nd
Have any accurate knowledge about the power line.	62%	46%	65%	67%	74%	70%
Say issue is "very important."	17%	13%	32%	42%	61%	64%
Say issue "affects me directly."	14%	10%	18%	12%	45%	43%

* 1st study   September, 1975
  2nd study   February, 1976

CONFLICT, IMPORTANCE, AND COLLECTIVE INTEREST

Other data relevant to the conflict-knowledge hypothesis include differences among subareas in the power-line study. Importance of the power-line topic and perceived conflict as measured by the "touchy subject" question differ sharply across community areas (Table 6-4). In both community O and community S areas, the highest importance ratings were in open

Table 6-4 Technical Knowledge and Perception of Conflict in
Power-Line Issue in two studies[*]

| | Community S | | | |
| | Metville | | Metfield | |
Percent Who:	(N:68) 1st	(N:48) 2nd	(N:39) 1st	(N:43) 2nd
Have heard of effects on health.	16%	8%	25%	26%
Have heard of effects on agriculture.	21%	8%	26%	23%
Have heard of under- ground installation.	28%	8%	28%	30%
Call topic a "touchy subject."	21%	23%	19%	51%

| | Community O | | | | | |
| | Town | | Rural area, East | | Rural area, Northwest | |
Percent who:	(N:71) 1st	(N:28) 2nd	(N:34) 1st	(N:33) 2nd	(N:31) 1st	(N:36) 2nd
Have heard of effects on health.	14%	29%	35%	39%	55%	67%
Have heard of effects on agriculture.	25%	42%	44%	48%	71%	70%
Have heard of under- ground installation.	32%	29%	41%	36%	68%	73%
Call topic a "touchy subject."	44%	33%	29%	36%	52%	83%

[*]1st study - September, 1975
2nd study - February, 1976

country locations and the lowest, particularly in the second
interviews, were in the communities with more concentrated
populations. The percent saying "very important" in the Metfield portion of community S jumped from 22% in the first
interviews to 46% in the second; a key event between the first
and second interview studies was a well-publicized meeting of
opposition groups in the community.

Such visible organizational activity as the opposition group meeting in Metfield is a key event in public arousal. Not only did perceived importance increase but also the direct impact on individuals was redefined. In Metfield, 22% of the respondents in the first interview said the issue "affects me directly"; in the second interview, after the new burst of organized opposition activity, more than twice as many (44%) answered the question affirmatively. Thus, the increases in perceived importance and perceived personal impact were almost perfectly parallel. This finding is particularly dramatic because in Metfield, the planned corridor routing remained unchanged between the first and second interview periods, since the entire community S area was near the "end point" of the line established months earlier in the power association and state agency announcements. Therefore, little new had occurred as far as power-line location was concerned. In light of that fact, the increased perception of importance and "direct effect" seems to be a direct outgrowth of organized activity and the intensity of conflict which that organization and its publicity produced.

The differences in perceived importance of the issue in the Metfield and Metville sections of community S may reflect differences in social structure. In the open-country areas of Metfield, where there is a lower degree of diversity, a problem in one rural sector is more likely to be seen as a problem by all in the area. In Metville, however, the greater population size and diversity means that the power-line issue was more likely to be submerged amid a variety of concerns and less likely to dominate public attention.

A further consequence of social structure can be seen in Table 6-3 by comparing the different parts of the community O area. In community O itself, the percentage rating of the power-line issue as "very important" dropped from 17% to 13% between the first and second interview. This is especially noteworthy, since the *Observer,* read by more than 90% of the community O town respondents, had given heavy attention to the issue and editorially opposed the power cooperatives, as described earlier. This finding indicates that neither heavy media coverage of an issue nor circulation could individually insure that people will see an issue as important. Judgments of importance also depend on how the issue is related to community self-interest. In this case, it appears that rural residents increasingly viewed the issue as a *general* rural area problem of individual rights, while town residents saw it in a quite different light. The town citizen may be more likely to see the problem as *primarily* one of energy needs, as might the urban citizen. The fact that the large urban media entered the reporting later, and editorialized as they did, seems to reflect this difference in problem definition. Such a similarity between small-town residents and the urban perspective may suggest that nonmetropolitan versus metropolitan differences may have a parallel in local farm-town divisions. Just as rural people tend to see things differently than big-city residents, so may similar differences exist at the local level between town and rural citizens.

WHERE PEOPLE GET INFORMATION ABOUT ISSUES

In both the regional planning and the power-line studies, respondents who had heard of the topic were asked, "Where have you seen or heard about this topic? Has it been from other persons, from television news, from radio news, from newspaper articles, or where?" Most of the sources mentioned were either newspapers or other persons, or a combination, a reflection of the dominance of newspaper publicity on both issues in the time period studied. The power line had not yet become a major television topic; television coverage started rather abruptly about four months after the second interviews, following heavy local coverage of the topic in the print media.

These data make it possible to test a hypothesis from the diffusion literature: Citizens tend to get their first information about a topic from mass media (in this case newspapers) rather than from personal contacts or sources. This hypothesis, frequently supported in studies of diffusion of information about farming practices and consumer goods, should also apply to knowledge about community-wide issues (North Central Regional Publication, 1955).

Evidence strongly supports the diffusion hypothesis (Figure 6-5). On the regional planning topic, the proportion citing newspapers, although quite low, is nevertheless higher in both communities than the proportion mentioning hearing it from other persons. But the most striking support for the hypothesis

Figure 6.5   Percent Getting Information from
Newspapers and from Talking with other Persons

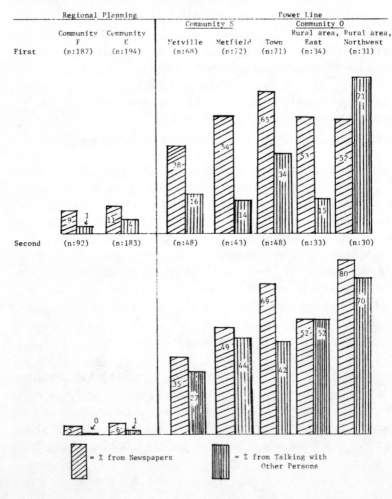

is in the results from the power-line issue, for which total
attention was much higher. In four of the five subareas of
communities O and S, the responses in the first interviews
indicate that percent seeing it in newspapers is higher than
percent hearing about it from other persons by at least 22
points. The one important exception is in the directly affected
area northwest of community O, where the issue was already
the dominant topic of conversation in the first interview. In
that area, organizational activity had been high with extensive
individual contacts concerning the issue; the potential impact of
the power line on local self-interest had already been discussed
in a highly organized setting.

In the second interviews, the sources of information patterns
as shown in Figure 6-5 are different. This time, percent talking
to others about the issue more nearly equaled the percent
reading about it in papers. In all areas except northwest of
community O, the proportion citing newspapers as sources of
information stays roughly the same as in the first interview and
citing other persons increases. In Metfield, mention of "other
persons" jumped from 14% in the first study to 44% in the
second, even though percent naming newspapers dropped
slightly, from 54% to 49%. In the area east of community O,
the increase in citing "other persons" was from 15% to 52%, so
that in the second interviews, proportions are identical for the
two sources. Seeking information from newspapers increased
sharply in only one area, northwest of community O where it
went from 52% to 80%.

The pattern in the power-line case may typify information
seeking and receiving for a variety of public affairs topics in
communities. People often get first word of events through the
media, unless an organization exists for transmitting the information through primary sources, as occurred in the northwest
townships. Most rural residents east of community O, who may
have been less likely to have friends or relatives directly involved with power-line negotiations in earlier months, apparently got their first information by reading about it. But as the
issue developed and the accompanying conflict and implications

for the rural area became more widely publicized, the matter became a topic for interpersonal communication. Newspaper reading, however, did not fall off; the results suggest that newspaper coverage may have reinforced, if not maintained, the levels of discussion. In some cases, conversation can stimulate increased reading, as may well have occurred in the northwest township. There, general involvement increased to a point where people may have sought still further information wherever they could find it.

NEWSPAPERS AND KNOWLEDGE

Since newspapers tend to be the most frequently cited source of information in both of the power-line studies, level of knowledge of the issue should differ according to the amount of newspaper reading. That expectation is supported (Table 6-5) when data for the second surveys in communities O and S are divided according to newspaper reading patterns. In both communities, the percent having any accurate knowledge about the issue is lowest for those persons who do *not* read the local

Table 6-5 Knowledge About the Power-Line Issue, According to Newspaper Reading in Two Communities

	Percent having *any* accurate knowledge about the issue
Community O area (metropolitan)	
Reads weekly *Observer*, but no metropolitan daily (n:24)	46%
Reads weekly *Observer* and also reads metropolitan daily (n:7)	14%
Does not read the weekly *Observer* (n:60)	7%
Community S area (rural)	
Reads weekly *Sentinel*, but no regional or metropolitan daily (n:44)	39%
Reads weekly *Sentinel* and also reads regional or metropolitan daily (n:15)	53%
Does not read weekly *Sentinel* (n:52)	21%

weekly paper. In rural community S, knowledge is highest among those who read both the weekly and a daily, whereas in community O, those who read the weekly but *not* a daily tend to be most knowledgeable about the issue. In the latter case, however, only seven respondents read both the weekly and a daily, so those results should be viewed with caution.

The findings do, however, indicate the importance of the weekly newspaper in these two communities and on this issue, since the lowest level of knowledge is among nonreaders in communities with weekly newspapers. These findings reflect again the fact that the weekly papers reported the issue as a community concern and from a community perspective.

MEASURES OF TECHNICAL KNOWLEDGE

The power-line study provides for an extensive examination of familiarity with, and knowledge about, various technical aspects of an issue. Several questions related to the proposed high-voltage power line which involved interpretation of a variety of technical arguments and scientific evidence. These questions fit largely into three categories—effects on health, effects on agriculture, and the question of underground installation.

The human health question was a prominent one, and was linked to a basic characteristic of the proposed line, "corona loss." Corona is an electric discharge around a power line that can vary according to weather conditions; corona loss is greater during rain, fog, and snow. The greater the corona loss, the greater the production of ozone and oxides of nitrogen. One of the frequently debated aspects of the power-line issue was the extent to which corona loss, through producing ozone, would present a danger to the health of workers around the line or to farm animals. Under certain weather and wind conditions, could ozone concentrate in certain areas at levels dangerous or perhaps fatal to livestock? The position of the cooperative power associations, supported by data supplied by their professional consultants (but challenged by opposition groups), was that the predictable concentrations of ozone and nitrogen oxides would pose no danger to humans or to livestock.

There were other health questions, such as whether the electric field would be injurious in other ways to persons working near the line for long periods of time. In various hearings, for example, there was a disagreement over translation of a Russian journal article summarizing a study of long-term effects of a high-voltage power line on workers. This journal article was cited frequently; at the time, very few places internationally had operated power lines with such high voltage (± 400 KV DC) for an appreciable period of time. The power association consultants at one hearing cited one translation of the Russian article which reported "disorders" of the functional state of the nervous and cardiovascular system of workers. Opposition groups cited a different translation of the same Russian journal article, which stated that a "shattering" of the central nervous system and cardiovascular system had occurred. Sharp and sometimes acrimonious exchanges over the various translations had occurred in the hearings.

Questions of effects on agriculture concerned such matters as amount of land taken up by the towers, inconvenience to farmers in working around towers and under the sag of the lines (130-foot towers, about 1,000 feet apart), potential difficulties for irrigation equipment and aerial crop spraying, and interference with activities in nearby farm buildings and yard areas.

The possibility of putting the high-voltage power line underground was raised frequently by individuals and farmer groups as an alternative solution to the controversy. Analyses published by the power associations claimed that problems in undergrounding a high-voltage transmission line are quite different from undergrounding lower voltage lines used in urban and residential areas and, therefore, opposed the alternatives as technically and economically unfeasible. One report from the power association stated that with current technology, undergrounding would require more than seven times as much steel and 10 times as much copper as overhead lines. Furthermore, the same report indicated that undergrounding would require high-pressure pipe-type systems, containing enormous amounts of oil. The power associations concluded that no undergrounding system, including the pipe-type, would be justifiable because of time, cost, and resource considerations. As a result, the power corridor hearings had proceeded on the assumption that the lines would be above ground, mounted on the large towers.

Other technical arguments arose, such as the potential effect on radio and television transmission. Health, agricultural, and underground installation concerns appeared to include the most frequently made statements, however, and these three points were utilized in the survey instruments. Respondents were asked: "Now we'd like to ask about three questions that have come up in connection with the power-line issue. One is the question of possible effects of high-voltage power lines on human health. Have you seen or heard of any scientific viewpoints or evidence about that?" If the respondent said yes, a probe was used to learn what the respondent had heard and where it had been heard. Similar questions were asked about possible effects on agriculture and about the possibility of underground installation. Other technical questions were also asked, such as the height of the poles, length of the line, and voltage.

KNOWLEDGE AND CONFLICT

Underlying this analysis of the special cases is the same basic hypothesis considered earlier: The higher the level of conflict surrounding an issue, the higher the level of citizen familiarity and knowledge concerning that issue. The test of that hypothesis, in the power-line case study, requires examination of data on the "touchy subject" question along with knowledge of individual technical issues (Table 6-4).

Findings about technical knowledge in the power-line issue are generally supportive of the conflict-knowledge hypothesis, that is, in areas where the subject is more likely to be viewed as touchy, knowledge on all counts tends to be highest (Table 6-4). Across all of the subareas studied, respondents in Metville

were among the least likely to term the issue "touchy"; that
subarea also displayed the lowest level of knowledge on all
aspects, including health, agriculture, underground installation,
and names of organizations and utilities. At the other extreme,
levels of knowledge on all of those aspects was highest in the
rural area northwest of community O where 52% in the first
wave and 83% in the second (highest both times) called the
issue touchy.

The relationship between perceived conflict and knowledge
can be illustrated graphically by plotting the percentages on the
touchy subject question against familiarity or knowledge.
Figure 6-6 (based on data appearing in Table 6-4) depicts the

Figure 6.6 Percent Calling Power Line Issue a "Touchy
Subject" and Percent Familiar with Underground
Installation in Five Sample Areas

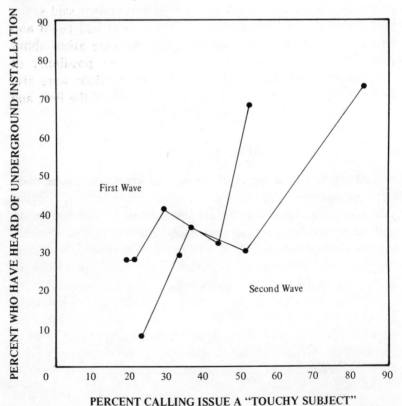

PERCENT CALLING ISSUE A "TOUCHY SUBJECT"

relationship for percent who have heard of underground installation. While the relationship is not perfectly linear, the clear tendency in both waves is for knowledge to be higher in areas where the topic is seen as more controversial. Furthermore, the line becomes straighter, and the differences in knowledge are more extreme, in the second wave of studies when the topic was seen as more touchy in all except one of the five areas.

One respect in which the data do not support the conflict-knowledge hypothesis is seen in Figure 6-6. The power-line issue was seen as more controversial in the second wave of interviews; yet, level of familiarity with underground installation in each of the five subareas was actually lower. The changing pattern of media coverage with more newspaper attention to the technical aspects of the problem in the early phases than in following months may be operating here. The controversy had reached a point where conflict *itself* was the major news item, as suggested above.

COMMUNITY ORGANIZATION, CONFLICT, AND KNOWLEDGE

The findings reported thus far in this chapter support the conflict-knowledge hypothesis but do not test directly the fundamental hypothesis: Conflict itself is generated as a result of organized social activity. A separate comparison of communities O, and S, characterized by high degrees of organized opposition, with 2 additional communities (not part of the 19) where lower degrees of organization surrounded the issue facilitated a test of the relationship in the 1977 power-line issue. This comparison also allows for a more direct test of the hypothesis that the higher the degree of organization surrounding an issue, the higher the public knowledge of that issue.

The comparison of two pairs of communities was made in a separate telephone interview study, in late winter and early spring of 1977, in communities O and S (high on organization) and the other two (low on organization) which we shall call T and U. The latter were selected for comparison for two reasons. First, community T, like S, is located within a metropolitan area, with a mixture of residential and open-country farm areas. Community U, like O, is a small town in a predominantly rural agricultural area. Second, as a result of participant observation, communities U and T were judged to have a lower degree of countervailing organization on the power-line dispute.

Communities T and U are geographically separated from O and S and are in what is called a *southern* region. They had their corridor hearings in 1976 and their route designation hearings in 1977, about a year later for each set of hearings than had occurred in O and S.

In neither community T nor U were there any organized demonstrations or confrontations associated with any of the hearings. No legal experts appeared at any of the hearings representing opposition groups, as had occurred in the central region where O and S are located. Also, community leaders and informants gave quite different impressions in the two regions. County extension agents, for example, in the central region regarded the opposition there as highly organized and intense. In the southern region, by contrast, the county agents regarded the issue as quiet and, as one put it, "quite unlike" the central region and without "very much organized opposition."

As a result, hearing testimony in the southern region took a different form. Whereas testimony in the central region was dominated by general and repeated questions of effects of the line, the southern region hearings particularly at the route hearings were characterized frequently by individuals speaking *as* individuals, seeking an alternation of the route that would benefit them alone.

When the route designation hearings were completed in the central region in 1976 with a state agency decision in favor of the power associations, the utilities began land surveying in the route area. This resulted in open confrontations between farmers and survey crews that summer on a number of farms near community O and in other areas along the line. A temporary injunction against further surveying was issued in the county in which O is located, but potentially violent incidents continued to occur throughout the summer of 1976. These incidents led to several requests for law enforcement personnel and the Minnesota National Guard to protect surveyors. A group of suits against the line project, originating in the central region, were pending in the state Supreme Court when the telephone interview were conducted in the late winter and early spring of 1977.

No demonstrations or major confrontations occurred in the southern region, and opposition groups issued few public state-ments about their positions on the issues, apart from some petitions at hearings. Although some organizations had mem-bers in both regions, public statements were made mostly by leaders in the central region. By comparison, the opposition in the southern region appeared much more quiescent.

NEWSPAPER CONTENT DIFFERENCES

During the two years prior to the 1977 interviews, the papers in communities S and O combined quoted or cited statements from opposition groups more than five times as frequently as did the papers in T and U combined. However, the S and O papers also quoted the power associations more often, some six times as frequently as in the T and U communities. This finding indicates that existence of countervailing organiza-tions led to increased coverage of their viewpoints. Indeed, if conflict is a state or condition of the system, this is to be expected. Intensity increased as a result of rising activity on the part of the power associations as well as among the opposing groups. In community O where coverage was heaviest, the number of statements attributed to the power associations and to opposition groups was almost exactly the same.

In addition, the weekly papers in communities O and S had more total coverage of the issue. In the two-year study period, these papers printed 1,823 and 848 column inches, respectively, on the issue. This compares with about 634 in community T and 571 in community U.

The metropolitan daily newspapers gave the power-line issue heavy coverage from June 1976 through the following winter.

The daily with the largest statewide circulation contained some 110 articles on the issue during the study period, and the topic was covered frequently as a major news item by television stations and radio stations around the state. At the end of 1976, one metropolitan television station termed the issue the "number two news story of the year," topped only by the taconite disposal issue of northeastern Minnesota, characterized also by organized groups with high levels of activity, including confrontation with government agencies and corporate groups.

ATTENTION, FAMILIARITY, AND KNOWLEDGE

Data in Table 6-6 are highly supportive of the hypothesis that the higher the degree of organization surrounding the issue, the greater the public knowledge. Citizens of the communities with higher levels of organization are more likely to have heard of the issue, to view it as controversial (i.e., as a touchy subject), and to display more knowledge about the issue, both in response to an open-end item and in response to specific items about potential effects of the power line on health and agriculture and about underground installation.

The assumption about greater communicative activity in communities O and S is generally supported (Table 6-7). Both of the communities with higher organizational levels show more respondents having heard about the topic from other persons, from television, and from reading newspapers. The one type of communicative activity not consistent with the assumption is hearing from radio, which occurred more frequently in community T (metropolitan area, lower level of organization) than in any other community, and lowest in community O (rural, higher level of organization). All communities are within range of metropolitan radio stations that gave the issue regular and frequent coverage during the previous year. Since local radio coverage was not monitored, no further explanation for the differences in radio listening is possible. However, it should also be pointed out that discussion of the issue was lowest in T, even though radio listening there was high.

Table 6-6 Perceptions of and Knowledge About the Power-Line Issue in Four Communities, 1977

	Communities with higher degrees of organization among opposition		Communities with lower degrees of organization among opposition	
	Community O (metropolitan) (n:200)	Community S (rural) (n:167)	Community T (metropolitan) (n:131)	Community U (rural) (n:149)
Percent who:				
Have heard of issue	84	88	63	68***
Rate issue as "very important"	47	67	38	54***
Call issue a "touchy subject"	64	78	42	54***
Know names of opposition organizations	14	26	4	13***
Make one or more accurate statements about power line issue (open end)	66	52	31	48***
Percent who have heard scientific evidence or viewpoints about:				
Questions of health	46	51	28	36***
Effects on agriculture	40	36	19	25***
Underground installation	55	44	32	38***

*** = difference across all groups, p < .001

Table 6-7 Sources of Information About the Power Line in Four Communities, 1977

	Communities with higher degrees of organization among interest groups		Communities with lower degrees of organization among interest groups	
	Community O (metropolitan) (n:200)	Community S (rural) (n:167)	Community T (metropolitan) (n:131)	Community U (rural) (n:149)
Percent who heard from:				
Other persons	34	50	28	31***
Television	67	61	44	50***
Newspapers	66	78	53	64***
Radio	39	26	56	30***
Percent who saw issue in local weekly paper	30	43	28	45**
Percent who saw issue in a daily newspaper	57	30	34	45***

** = difference across all groups, p < .01
*** = difference across all groups, p < .001

Patterns of recall of the issue in weeklies and dailies vary from one community to another, although these differences are not extreme. As indicated in Table 6-7, percent seeing the issue mentioned in a weekly is highest in the two most rural communities (O and U). Recall from a daily is highest in the metropolitan area community S and lowest in O. The daily most frequently mentioned in communities, S, O, and T is the largest metropolitan newspaper in the state. In community U, the most frequently mentioned daily newspaper source is from a regional urban center about 25 miles away.

In general, then, the date offer considerable support for the hypothesis that degree of organization among countervailing groups is associated with higher community levels of awareness and knowledge about all aspects of the issue. The one finding that is not entirely in line with the hypothesis is the rating of importance of the issue; the rating (Table 6-6) in community U (rural, lower level of organization) is higher than in community O (metro, higher organizational level). However, when comparisons are made between structurally similar communities, the importance ratings are, predictably, higher in O than in T and higher in S than in U.

SUMMARY

Understanding the process of social conflict is basic to understanding the generation and spread of knowledge in a community. Conflict grows out of countervailing social groups seeking to reach their respective goals within the system. Conflict frequently gives rise to increased mass media publicity, which in turn tends to accelerate the intensity of the conflict.

As intensity rises, interpersonal communication about the issue increases among people in groups creating higher general levels of knowledge among the groups within the community. In this process, the impact of the newspapers is indirect, and the specific role of the newspapers may change as the issue develops. As expected from diffusion theory, citizens tend to get their first information about an issue from the mass media. The relative importance of interpersonal communication as a source increases with time and duration of the conflict. Even at high levels of intensity, however, newspapers and other mass media continue to receive high attention. At intense stages, reciprocal effects among media and discussion with other persons may occur. That is, reading may stimulate conversation, and conversation about a topic may stimulate the citizenry to pay more attention to future news about the topic.

Conflict is related not only to familiarity with an issue but also to technical knowledge about the issue. The more intense the conflict about the power line in different geographical areas, the more the respondents in those areas tended to know about technical aspects of the topic.

In general, the conflict-knowledge hypothesis receives considerable support from the data. At the same time, the data do not support the view that "nobody learns anything" in a conflict. It may well be that possession of technically incorrect information may *also* increase in a heavily publicized and intense situation. But what is often seen as misinformation in a conflict situation may be an aspect of conflict itself. By their nature, conflicts are characterized by differing interpretations of evidence and reality, and these differing interpretations may come from technical and scientific experts as well as from other observers. To be knowledgeable about the scope of a community conflict is to be aware of these differing perspectives, and the evidence supports the conclusion that such knowledge does increase as intensity increases.

REFERENCES

BOGARDUS, E. S. (1920) Essentials of Social Psychology. Los Angeles: University of California Press.

COLEMAN, J. S., E. KATZ, and H. MENZEL (1966) Medical Innovation: A Diffusion Study. Indianapolis, IN: Bobbs-Merrill.

COSER, L. A. (1967) Continuities in the Study of Social Conflict. New York: Macmillan.

––– (1956) The Functions of Social Conflict. New York: Macmillan.

DAHRENDORF, R. (1959) Class and Class Conflict in Industrial Society. Palo Alto, CA: Stanford University Press.

FEAGIN, J. R. (1974) "Issues in welfare research: a critical overview." Social Science Quarterly 54: 321-328.

GRAHAM, H. D. (1967) Crisis in Print: Desegregation and the Press in Tennessee. Nashville: Vanderbilt University Press.

KATZ, E. (1955) Personal Influence. New York: Macmillan.

LIPPMANN, W. (1922) Public Opinion. New York: Macmillan.

LUNDBERG, G. A. (1939) The Foundations of Sociology. New York: Macmillan.

North Central Regional Publication (1955) How Farm People Accept New Ideas (Report 1). Ames: Iowa State College Agricultural Extension Service.

OBENG-QUAIDOO, I. (1977) "Hutterite land expansion and the Canadian press." Ph.D. dissertation, University of Minnesota.

ROGERS, E. M. (1962) Diffusion of Innovations. New York: Macmillan.

TICHENOR, P. J. and D. WACKMAN (1973) "Mass media and community public opinion." American Behavioral Scientist 16: 593-606.

7

Conflict
and the
Knowledge Gap

It happened in Cincinnati shortly after World War II. A coalition of civic organizations with cooperation of radio stations and newspapers and scores of local groups was determined to raise the level of citizen knowledge about the United Nations. Their object was to demonstrate "how a community may become so intelligently informed on world affairs as to be a dynamic force in the creation of an ordered and eventually a peaceful world."

They organized an intensive information campaign directed toward the entire 1.1 million population in the Cincinnati trade area. Newspapers agreed to "play up" the United Nations for six months. Radio stations broadcast facts, one doing as many as 150 spot announcements in a single week. Some 60,000 pieces of literature were distributed; Parent Teacher Associations reached 13,000 people; every student was given literature on the United Nations to take home to parents; a speakers bureau reached 2,800 clubs; civic organizations throughout the community viewed hundreds of documentary films.

To evaluate the campaign, the sponsoring groups arranged for a survey of Cincinnati adults in September 1947 before the campaign began, with a follow-up survey of the same respondents in March 1948, after the campaign had run for six months. Respondents in each survey were given a six-item information test.

The results showed clearly that the stated goals were not reached: 15% got five or six of the items right in September, with the same percentage scoring that high in March. It was not that nobody was reached by the campaign; it was a question of *who* was reached. In the words of the authors of the study, the audience reached by the campaign was primarily "the better educated, the younger and the men—precisely the people most likely to be interested and, being interested, also to be informed." For example, 68% of the college-educated in March said they had seen information about the campaign in three or more places. That compares with 43% of those with a high school education and only 17% of those having no formal education beyond the grade school level (Star and Hughes, 1950).

Such experiences have been repeated in many communities and on many subjects. A group of professional educators in Norway used an eight-part television series to promote books among children 2 to 10 years old. Since they were attempting to reduce social class differences in the buying of books among children, they used lively "commercials" to stimulate children to ask their parents to buy the books.

Instead of attracting a large audience of working class children, however, the commercials had an effect similar to the Cincinnati campaign. Only 3% of the children in working class families received the books, according to a follow-up survey. In middle-class families, 16% bought the books, more than five times the proportion of working class children.

Conclusions reached by the Norwegian educators may be familiar today in extension programs, community development, and preschool education as well:

> The intended effect of the television campaign was to diminish differences between children from different strata . . . however, the actual result was quite the opposite; the campaign contributed to increasing the "knowledge gap" [Werner, 1975: 50].

Social science literature on information campaigns and educational programs is now replete with results similar to those from the Cincinnati and Norwegian experiences. Researchers and program evaluators in a wide range of situations, in a number of different cultures, have often found such campaigns and communication efforts producing everwidening knowledge gaps between more and less educated groups, or between high- and low-status groups generally. Such findings seem to contradict directly a cherished assumption of educational campaigns: Increasing the flow of information will lead to greater equalization of knowledge throughout the system. The recent data indicate that the question is not so much one of increasing knowledge, but, frequently, one of relative deprivation of knowledge. Several studies now support the hypothesis that as the flow of information into a social system increases, segments of the population with higher levels of education often acquire this information at a faster rate than segments with low education. As a result, gaps in knowledge between these segments tend to increase rather than decrease (Tichenor, Donohue, and Olien, 1970). Knowledge of space research is an example; after several years of heavy national media attention to space rocketry and satellites, the gap in knowledge about the topic across educational levels was greater than it had been before the space research program began. Similarly, knowledge gaps widened over time for the smoking and cancer issue.

SOCIAL STRUCTURE, KNOWLEDGE GAPS, AND SOCIAL CONTROL

Within a social control framework, knowledge gaps are predictable outcomes of existing patterns of distribution and acquisition of knowledge (Donohue, Tichenor, and Olien, 1975). Within any total social system, some subsystems have patterns of behavior and values conducive to change, while others have patterns that are more resistant to change. These patterns are maintained and reinforced by institutions and specific agencies that distribute services and resources differentially, so that those with the more change-conducive values and behavioral patterns are more likely to undergo still further change. The outcome with information is comparable to outcome with any social resource. The predisposed subsystems tend to acquire, adopt, and act upon information at a faster rate than the more stagnant subsystems. In the case of the Cincinnati campaign and most campaigns like it, the involvement of such organizations as Parent Teacher Associations and civic groups directs the information immediately toward more highly educated persons, since their leadership and membership tend generally to be above average on this variable. Interest in world organizations is generally a concern of the more highly educated; similarly, interest in books is more likely to be a developed orientation in the middle-class Norwegian homes than in those lower in the social class structure.

Differential patterns of distribution and acquisition of knowledge have major consequences for social control and social stratification. They tend to maintain existing elites of specialized groups within the social structure. Even if members of lower status positions see the information as relevant, they are less able to interpret it or apply it in furtherance of their own interests.

Social control implications of differential distribution and acquisition of knowledge may be highly apparent in some situations but more subtle in others. Consider the implications for two individuals in a community, one a college-trained engineer and the other a high-school dropout working as a supermarket clerk, both of whom are *potentially* exposed to a newspaper report about the power-line controversy which includes the following information:

> A superconductor able to operate near room temperature, though a distant and perhaps impossible goal, would revolutionize electrical technology. One obvious use for superconductors is in electrical transmission lines. The massive overhead power cables, the center of the current controversy, could be replaced by a single, more efficient superconductor strand. . . . A variety of other uses for superconductors is being considered. Superconductor electromagnets are thought to be essential in forming magnetic "bottles," the key to

fusion power. Fusion power (not to be confused with fission power, currently the only form of nuclear energy) is thought to be a safer and cleaner way to generate power than present nuclear power plants.

From a professional writing point of view, this excerpt and the article from which it is taken might rate rather well as examples of comprehensible technical description. But what are the communication processes, within a given community structure, that determine the audience impact? One might argue at first blush that for a college-trained engineer the article "tells nothing new" and that the clerk is the only one of the two who stands to gain new information.

But consider the circumstances more closely. The engineer, as a college graduate, is more likely to subscribe to the paper and scan the content than is the clerk. So at the very first point of contact, potential self-exposure tends to favor the engineer. Nevertheless, assume next that both engineer and clerk see the article. Even then, the clerk is less likely to recognize the term *superconductors*, even though it was explained earlier in the article. For the engineer, superconductivity is a term that he may recall from one or more college courses, from the professional literature, from trade magazines, from meetings, or from conversations with other engineers. Although the excerpt may tell the engineer little that is new in a technical sense, what is there is comprehensible and fits into his current state of knowledge. If the clerk reads through the article far enough to reach this particular passage, he is unlikely to retain more than the idea of a "distant solution" to the controversy.

The communication processes do not necessarily stop at this point. The engineer has regular contacts with other engineers and technical specialists who have various kinds of expert knowledge about power lines and new developments in high-power transmission. If the power-line topic comes up in conversation between the engineer and his peers, someone in the group is likely to recall and be able to relate the news report to some part of the professional body of knowledge. Such a discussion may even stimulate an engineer who has not already seen the news report to seek it out. Because of his organizational contacts and his status as a professional, the engineer is in a stream of correspondence, professional journals, and industrial and trade magazines which have previously alerted him to, and kept him reminded of, the idea of superconductivity.

For the clerk, the likelihood of encountering a working associate with such specialized knowledge is far more remote. Since he deals with a variety of persons, the clerk may at some point talk with, say, an electrician whose knowledge about the subject goes well beyond that of the lay person. But even here, the electrician's knowledge compared with that of a college-trained engineer is likely to be limited to experience and contemporary installation. A practicing technician, because of the information delivery systems in the specialized professions, is far less likely than the professional specialist to be located in a flow of communication that keeps him or her abreast of emerging scientific research in the field.

The possibility exists that the clerk will see the information about superconductors and will encounter other individuals and other sources of information that will reinforce and/or interpret what was in that newspaper article. But, given the way production and dissemination of specialized information occurs within the system, the *probabilities* of such exposure, follow-up discussions, and interpretation are overwhelmingly greater for the professional engineer.

The structurally different capacities of the engineer and supermarket clerk to understand the superconductivity report in the newspaper go beyond the technical aspects of the topic. The professional engineer is also in a better position to interpret the report in a social or political action context. As an engineer, his regular contact with professional literature and professional persons exposes him to a parallel stream of information about agencies, corporations, and other organizations that utilize engineering information. A highly active professional is also likely to be aware of "the politics" of the field; he is more likely to know what is "behind the story" (Sigal, 1973). Interpretations of professional information are often controversial precisely because of their social and political ramifications. The clerk may well regard the power-line issue as a "political" one, but, surrounded at work and at home by others with limited training and education, his social location provides neither informal nor specialized information about the intricacies of agency and corporate activity relating to the topic. The clerk does not necessarily lack the ability to comprehend those intricacies; it is his location in the structure that reduces the likelihood that details or interpretations will ever reach him and make sense in his frame of reference. Whether it is a matter of conscious design or not, the structure is such that the clerk's understanding of the superconductivity report is likely to be controlled at a minimal level, while the engineer's understanding is controlled at a maximal level.

This outcome would not necessarily become apparent from asking the engineer and the clerk to evaluate the article. The engineer might be quick (as specialists in the power-line study were) to say the article on superconductivity "told me nothing I didn't know already." In terms of the basic principle or applicability of that concept, the engineer may be correct in that assessment, whereas the clerk might respond that the article "has an interesting idea, one I hadn't heard before." However, the very fact of prior familiarity means the engineer can quickly grasp the fact of the article—such research is being done—and its relevance for the entire issue. Therefore, a test of comprehension would be expected to give results quite different from the respective evaluations; as studies such as those by Funkhouser and Maccoby (1973) indicate, the expert tends to comprehend more from popularized articles than does the nonexpert.

Differential impact of information on the engineer and the clerk is not limited to the more extensive discussions of superconductors. A far more superficial treatment of the subject might have a similar widening effect on the knowledge gap. The engineer is in a better position in the system to see implications of the most minimal information and to act on that information if he so desires. He, and not the clerk, is in a better position to write or telephone the research team studying conductors. The engineer, as a result of his college training, is more familiar with academic research institutions and is more likely to know the specialized language and to have direct access to a center of specialized research. The clerk, by comparison, is more likely to see the university research center as a more socially distant place, perhaps highly prestigious, but not one that he would consider approaching directly on this particular topic. The relationship between social position and contact with centers of higher learning has been documented by Johnstone (1965), for example, who found that students seeking adult education were heavily concentrated in upper income and educational groups. Persons who had already succeeded at school and in professional positions came to school to learn still more.

In the above illustration, we have been discussing social roles in the form of engineer and clerk and not individual personalities, a point which is central to the knowledge gap hypothesis. Even though they are played by individuals, roles are defined and developed as part of the structure and not on the basis of idiosyncratic behavior of persons playing roles at any given point in time.

SYSTEM FACTORS AND THE KNOWLEDGE GAP

Massive portions of the knowledge generation and distribution industry, both in the United States and in most other parts of the world, are oriented toward persons with higher education. Even the most primitive form of newspaper, for example, requires basic literacy. But a minimal ability to read is usually not enough for coping with a newspaper, and newspaper circulation departments do not necessarily seek out groups of citizens with low levels of reading ability or with low levels of income that make them lesser targets for advertisements. Newspapers value high-status information sources such as those in education, science, and cultural reporting. The less-educated person who reads a newspaper is more likely to confine his or her reading to content other than public affairs information, whereas the information about politics, science, culture, and the arts is more frequently read by persons with higher levels of education (Davis, 1958; Schramm and Wade, 1967; Samuelson, Carter, and Ruggels, 1963; Robinson, 1967; Westley and Severin, 1963).

Furthermore, the less educated person who reads a newspaper is more likely to be limited to a newspaper published locally. Nearly 50 years ago, Lynd and Lynd (1929) found 3 of every 5 business class families in Middletown taking an out-of-town newspaper, compared with only 1 in every 50 working class families. The social control implications are clear in the authors' statement that "such differential diffusion is the stuff of which the habitual reactions of the group are to no inconsiderable extent formed."

Several other observers contend that the orientation of newspapers and other print media toward more highly educated segments of the community is part of a total structure of institutional arrangements and normative patterns maintaining patterns of inequality by favoring the position of the more powerful groups in society (Suominen, 1976). Gerbner and Gross (1976) view the primary function of television as constantly reiterating the legitimacy, and maintenance, of established power and authority. Some evidence suggests that members of less advantaged groups tend to subscribe to, and therefore reinforce, the same norms (Rainwater, 1969).

STATUS FLOW IN PLANNED COMMUNICATION PROGRAMS

The knowledge gap phenomenon has several parallels in social action programs generally. The excitement and enthusiasm of the War on Poverty during the 1960s eventually gave way to the more realistic conclusion that projects often fail to meet their fundamental objectives of reducing the gaps in achievement. While such projects as Head Start, Model Cities, and others may have led to improvements for disadvantaged groups in an absolute sense, evidence of their success in improving the position of disadvantaged groups *relative* to other groups in society is less apparent. Mandelbaum (1972), in an especially blunt appraisal, argues that "elite attempts to control the barbarians have taken many forms," and sees propaganda, coercion, and questionable uses of welfare payments as having similar control consequences. He contends that urban antipoverty programs, including the communication portion of these programs, serve to maintain rather than alter existing power relationships and centers of control. He states:

> Underlying all of the talk and the shouting about decentralization, neighborhood control, citizen participation and new politics, is the search for a new synthesis of institutions and relationships. . . . In fact, the counterattack so far has succeeded only where it promises to extend elite security rather than to imperil it. Community control in inner-city neighborhoods is fine as long as it leaves the suburbs in command of their own resources [1972: 98].

As with many resources in action programs, knowledge is typically generated, distributed, and controlled in ways that direct it to groups that can most easily and effectively take advantage of it.

Three mechanisms of control over knowledge may be identified, including control over *access, distribution,* and *reinforcement.* Control over *access* to information is often based upon knowledge generated by groups oriented toward self-maintenance and more highly educated strata generally. Nearly any professional or scientific group may be taken as an example. Generation and accumulation of knowledge is fundamental to growth and development of a specialized field. A scientific discipline feels it has arrived when it possesses a unique body of knowledge which is considered necessary and can be dispensed to the other segments of society in a therapeutic fashion. To be an "authority" is high acclaim for a scientist, as Hagstrom (1965) has pointed out. Procedures of scientific and academic disciplines for review and criticism serve as deviancy control mechanisms at the level of the scientific subsystem. These procedures may be referred to as socially patterned differentials in access to new knowledge (Merton, 1972), possession of which separates an "insider" from an "outsider." In the power-line corridor hearings described earlier, the sharp disputes over credibility of translations of a Russian journal article had implications well beyond the question of whether power lines are in fact injurious to human health. The disputes drew attention to the fact that access to such literature depends heavily on one's connections with the scientific organizations that publish it.[1]

Given the First Amendment and the values which Americans place on free speech and unrestricted dissemination of information, one might argue that the prevailing value system would produce a degree of equalization of information access. However, even though status flow is related to such values and to their implementation, other values and structures may be equally important in determining who has access to specialized information. As Gerbner and Gross (1976) indicate, powerful values about social control exert a great deal of pressure on the definition of communication and therefore on the consequences of its dissemination in the system.

Within the structure, differential tastes for content among groups occupy different status positions. Content which generally appeals differentially to lower status groups includes comics, personal advice columns, and other forms of entertainment content. Such content is referred to by some critics (e.g., DeFleur, 1966) as "low-taste" content. From a structural perspective, low-taste content is the "opiate of the people" - media's response not to the needs of the lower status groups but to the supposed needs of the upper status groups to maintain control. Therefore, criticism of certain media content as "low taste" may itself reinforce knowledge gaps by maintaining differential access. Such criticism is itself a form of social control since it tends to reinforce negative definitions of content, even if that content continues to appear in media at a steady rate. These negative definitions may strengthen the tendency of higher status groups to expose themselves selectively to what they regard as "serious" content, including public affairs information. Content which carries with it a negative definition frequently serves to further reinforce the lower status of its adherents and, therefore, their lower degree of social power.

Control over *distribution* is closely related to control over access. Warren (1973) has noted the ability of community decision-making organizations (which tend to be dominated by the highly educated segments) to control the communications media through which social problems are defined and in which intervention strategies are stated and discussed. In development programs generally, high-status groups tend to plan and control distribution of programs. Such control appears to persist in spite of various attempts to "involve" members of less-educated segments in planning. After studying educational television programming in a number of developing nations, one observer was moved to comment that he had "not found a case where members of minority or nondominant social and cultural groups have participated in curriculum planning and development" (Arnove, 1975). For the most part, Arnove says the urban elite had joined forces with ex-colonial powers to plan and develop educational television programming. Similar patterns of control are noted frequently in the United States, one of the most recent cases being the introduction of contemporary textbooks in elementary schools. These printed materials are usually advocated and distributed by college-trained professional educators whose urban values often conflict sharply with, and override, those of substantial segments of rural communities (Cummings, Briggs, and Mercy, 1977).

Even if information access and distribution *are* relatively equalized, differential patterns of reinforcement for acquiring that information may depress the extent to which less-educated groups find it and use it. As with the case of the fictional engineer and clerk above, enthusiasm for information results from being in situations where that information is talked about and the individual is likely to be asked about it. The importance of such reinforcement was noted specifically by Chu (1968) in a study of four traditional communities in Taiwan. Chu found that even among media *users*, farmers low on economic status and whose social contacts were limited to other low-status persons were seldom consulted by others seeking their advice or interpretation of media content. This "withdrawal of social reward," Chu found, contributed to the lesser use of media by low-status villagers. The result was that well-off and more highly educated farmers were able to maintain their high status by using media to update themselves on relevant information.

The combined effects of differential distribution and access to information, and differential reinforcement among recipients, have been especially apparent in many extension programs in rural areas, both in the United States and in developing nations. Consequences for knowledge gaps have been noted in recent years by a number of observers. Rogers (1976), for example, regards the "communications effect gap" as a pervasive consequence of development activities and concludes that if more equitable distribution of benefits is a goal of development, unconventional communication strategies are required. Rolig, Ascroft, and WaChege (1976) reach similar conclusions, finding that inequities often emerge in previously egalitarian societies as a result of diffusion of innovations. McNelly (1973) is one of several who have questioned whether the "two-step flow" of information from leaders to less-active segments does in fact operate in information programs in developing nations. The "Green Revolution," many of these observers conclude, primarily benefited larger farmers in developing countries and therefore widened knowledge gaps and resultant socioeconomic benefits. Some specialists have concluded that if equalization of information is a goal, developing countries should consider information programs producing content that advantaged farmers already understand but which would be new to less-advantaged farmers (Shingi and Mody, 1976). However, in view of the above discussion of the different roles of the engineer and clerk, such information programs may not achieve their intended outcome. The structure in which the citizen operates is determinative, not the knowledge per se.

THE KNOWLEDGE GAP AND COMMUNITY FACTORS

While there are now extensive data that support the knowledge gap hypothesis, the findings and explanations raise a question of major social significance. Under what conditions, if any, might this knowledge gap be reduced or eliminated?

Several social system variables may affect either the existence of knowledge gaps or their magnitude. One of these factors is *structure,* particularly the degree of pluralism or homogeneity as discussed in some detail in previous chapters. A second is the *nature of the issue,* particularly the extent to which it engages basic concerns in a social system. A third is the level of *system conflict* accompanying the general social definition of the issue in question. Data from the 19 communities may be examined, treating these factors as independent variables and the knowledge gap as a dependent variable.

BASIC CONCERNS AND SOCIAL CONFLICT

If knowledge gaps widen as the flow of information appealing to concerns of specialized groups increases, then that tendency to widen should theoretically be reduced to the extent that information appeals to more basic concerns in a social system. An example of a basic social concern might be general attachment to a community and to its survival and maintenance. These concerns could be aroused where such issues as community modernization, urban renewal, or environmental restrictions on local industry are involved. Arousal of basic concerns may be accompanied by varying levels of conflict, or tension arising from awareness of differing public positions between groups, either within the community or between the community and some outside agency or another community.

Social conflict about a topic of basic concern may have positive functions for arousal and maintenance of citizen participation, as discussed in earlier chapters. Conflict may be related to total communicative activity in a number of ways, depending on the structure of the system, and it should theoretically have important consequences for the knowledge gap. Under certain conditions the relationship between conflict and the knowledge gap might be linear and positive, while under other conditions it might be linear and negative or even curvilinear. A point might be reached where conflict is so intense and rancorous that it becomes the issue, rather than the original topic. Communication itself, in such cases, frequently shifts to interpersonal channels. When the power-line issue reached explosive proportions, several community leaders tried to initiate negotiations "behind the scenes," out of the glare of publicity. This tendency can occur whether the conflict is within the community or between segments of the community and an outside agency as in the power-line issue.

At what point will conflict produce what is popularly called a "communication breakdown," and therefore a shift in communicative strategies? Specifically, the answer to that question is a matter for empirical determination, but in theory it is a point where the tension is widely interpreted as reaching a level where a rupture in the established social order is seen as imminent. When angry protest groups face each other or groups of police for the first time, the prospect for violence is new, frightening, and portending of a breakdown of conventional social stability. Up to that point, to the extent that conflict draws attention to basic social concerns, it should direct attention to the issue throughout that community. The result is to overcome, at least partially, some of the selective dissemination and self-exposure patterns that contribute to knowledge gap widening on topics of specialized interest. Since tension up to the point of a breakdown is a stimulant to public communicative activity, it might be expected to reduce the knowledge gap, at least to a lower magnitude than if less conflict surrounded the issue. Presence of conflict, then, would be expected to increase the probability that the gap will be reduced, since there is likely to be a greater arousal of widespread concern than might occur without conflict.

Consequences of social conflict for the reduction of knowledge gaps might be considered for the case of the college-trained engineer and the clerk, cited earlier. If they live in a community where the power line is a central issue, the local newspaper is more likely to display articles about the issue in prominent locations, with bold headlines. Such coverage is likely to recur frequently over months and years. Such concentrated attention increases the likelihood that a particular news article will be seen by the clerk and the engineer alike; it is a topic people are likely to mention in conversation.

Wide exposure to such news does not, by itself, eliminate the knowledge gap between the clerk and the engineer, but the stimulation of an intense conflict *is* likely at least to reduce the magnitude of the gap from that of a more distant issue. If the issue is a "hot topic," the clerk is more likely to become familiar with it than if it were regarded as quite remote. Learning may well be reinforced in such situations by discussion, which is itself more likely in conflict situations. The rank correlation between conflict and interpersonal communication, across 24 community issues, as indicated in Chapter 6 is .50 (p < .05). In addition, it should be added that the rank correlation between interpersonal communication and the knowledge gap coefficient is -.58 (p < .01). It seems quite clear that the more the stimulation of the formal and informal communication channels in the community accompanying the intensity of a conflict situation, the more equalized the distribution of information across educational segments will be.

An illustration of the effects of national conflict on knowledge gaps is the Watergate issue, in which the question of criminal behavior in the White House may well have touched a fundamental concern of Americans generally. The episode was characterized by some of the most concentrated newspaper and broadcast publicity of any national issue short of war. Some evidence suggests that the heavy coverage and intensity of the conflict situation, resulted in low correlations between knowledge of the Watergate episode and education of citizens (Neuman, 1976). Chaffee and Becker (1975) reported almost identical levels of broadcast exposure to Watergate news, regardless of education, in a Madison, Wisconsin, sample. To a considerable extent, the knowledge gap closed on that issue.

COMMUNITY STRUCTURE AND THE KNOWLEDGE GAP

The degree of pluralism characteristic of a community structure is directly relevant to the knowledge gap hypothesis. Pluralism, by definition, involves differentiation and specialization of roles and functions. Therefore, the greater the community pluralism, the greater the possibilities for widening the knowledge gaps between different social strata within the community. The more pluralistic a community, the more sources of formal and informal information it contains, and the more selective the patterns of self-exposure among its members. On the other hand, the more homogeneous the community, the fewer the specialized media and the more the dependency on interpersonal communication patterns. In a smaller and more homogeneous community, the likelihood that the "whole town will talk" about a topic of basic concern is much greater. Such universal discussion would theoretically tend to equalize information flow across status lines and narrow the knowledge gap. In the case cited above, if the power-line and the undergrounding questions are tension-laden topics that come up frequently and repeatedly in everyday conversation, the clerk will very likely be in a situation where the topics are mentioned and discussed. In a homogeneous community situation, such conversations are likely to occur in a variety of settings.

Community structure and conflict may be seen as interdependent variables which may have joint effects on patterns of acquisition of information. That is, a given type of conflict may become widespread more quickly in a more homogeneous community. For example, in a single industry town, conflict about employment issues would be heightened more rapidly than it would in a more diversified, pluralistic city where there are multiple sources of employment and economic support. In the latter case, a severe depression leading to general unemployment would tend to heighten such awareness.

EVIDENCE ON CONFLICT AND THE KNOWLEDGE GAP

Data on the knowledge gap question are taken from all 19 communities studied. As with previous analyses, knowledge level for each community issue is determined according to the number of accurate statements which the community respondents make. Level of conflict is measured according to the same responses described earlier. That is, in all of the communities, the open-ended knowledge responses were examined to determine whether the respondents mentioned any type of conflict among persons or groups when asked what he or she "had seen or heard" about the topic recently. In 16 of the communities, an additional measure was used: Respondents in those cases were asked "Would you say the question of [issue under study] is a touchy subject around here, or not?" Proportion saying yes is taken as an indicator of level of perceived conflict in the community. In the 16 cases where both measures were used, the Spearman rank correlations between the two is .65 (p < .01).

The knowledge gap for a given community is measured in one of two ways, depending upon the characteristics of the data. One measure is the Pearsonian correlation coefficient between level of education and level of knowledge about an issue. Another, in cases where knowledge distributions are highly skewed, is the difference in proportion having a certain level of knowledge, e.g., between the college-educated group and those with less than college education.

A NONLOCAL ISSUE AND THE KNOWLEDGE GAP

According to the revised knowledge gap hypothesis, increasing information flow should be positively related to increasing knowledge gaps on issues which are nonlocal and do not arouse basic social concerns. In four of the communities studied, a national issue had been in the news during the three months preceding the interviews. The issue was the nutritive value of breakfast cereals; the news had been directed almost entirely toward congressional hearings and the breakfast food industry in general. Virtually no implications for any particular community existed. However, attention to the issue in local newspapers had varied sharply, providing a direct test of the knowledge gap hypothesis.

The basic hypothesis as originally stated is supported by data on the breakfast food issue (Figure 7-1). As newspaper attention to this issue increases, so does the magnitude of the

Figure 7.1   Newspaper Coverage Index and Strength of
Correlation Between Education and Knowledge for the
Breakfast Cereal Issue in Four Communities

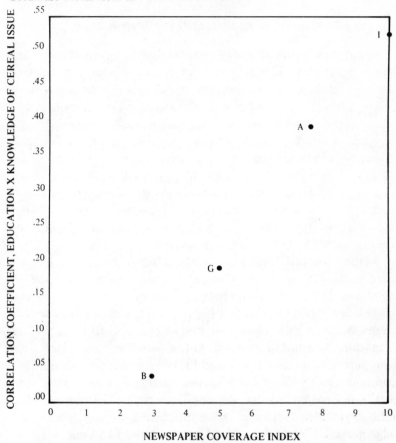

positive correlation between education and knowledge. Differences in the sizes of these correlations are marked, ranging from
a low of .05 in community B, where the topic received the least
coverage, to .51 in community I, where it received nearly three
times as much coverage. These four communities are very similar in size with populations varying from 8,300 to 9,900 and all
are agricultural trade centers with similar characteristics, thus
controlling for pluralism in this particular analysis. These findings lend further support to the proposition that on national
issues involving no immediate consequences for communities,

increasing media coverage leads to greater differentials in knowledge across educational status groups.

CONFLICT, LOCAL ISSUES, AND THE KNOWLEDGE GAP

If data on national issues support the basic knowledge gap hypothesis, what about knowledge on local issues? Results of analyses of local issues portray a quite different pattern of relationship. For the 19 Minnesota communities as a whole, the size of the knowledge gap was only weakly related to the newspaper coverage index and in a negative direction. The rank correlation between these two variables for the 19 communities, across 27 issues, is −.34 (nonsignificant). That is, the knowledge gap between education segments tends to be slightly narrower where there is heavier media input. These findings suggest that the original hypothesis, however well supported by previous data, may not hold for all situations.

Among the variables that might contribute to a lower knowledge gap may be level of conflict surrounding the issue in question. The relationship between perceived conflict and the knowledge gap is indicated in Figure 7-2. The correlation coefficients between education and knowledge tend to be of higher magnitude in communities where the issues are associated with low perceived conflict. Among the 5 "low perceived conflict" communities (10% or less viewing the issue as a "touchy subject"), 4 have knowledge gap coefficients of .25 or higher. The rank correlation between the conflict measure and the knowledge gap coefficient for the 12 communities (15 issues) is −.61 (p < .01), which is rather strong support for the hypothesis that as conflict level increases, the knowledge gap in a community decreases.

Data in Figure 7-2 reflect the importance of both the conflict dimension and the extent to which the issue arouses basic concerns. The knowledge gap has the greatest magnitude on the regional development issue, an issue of low general concern, in two similar communities, G and A. This issue arose with the 1969 Minnesota Regional Planning Act, which laid the groundwork for establishing regional development commissions. Less than a year before the surveys in four of these communities were conducted, the governor delineated the boundaries of 11 such regions in Minnesota. Formation of regional development commissions was to be accomplished voluntarily at the local level. The issue had received some publicity—at a level about average for the various issues in the study as a whole. Regional development, however, had not been viewed as a major issue by the population as a whole; in none of the four communities where it was studied did more than 17% view it as "very important."

Community R provides an illustration of the consequences of high intensity versus low intensity surrounding an issue, since two quite different issues were studied there. One issue was a nuclear power plant, which had been the center of a statewide controversy over safety standards about three years previous to

Figure 7.2 Percent Perceiving Issue as "Touchy Subject" and Strength of Correlation between Education and Knowledge in 15 Community Issue Comparisons

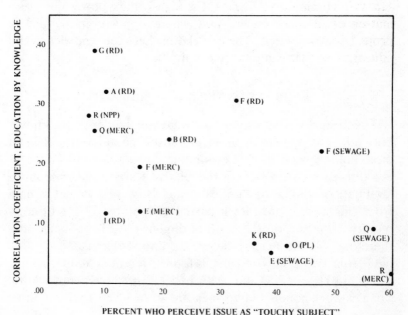

PERCENT WHO PERCEIVE ISSUE AS "TOUCHY SUBJECT"

the survey. Only a fourth of the community R respondents regarded the power plant as "very important"; it was a low-conflict issue and the knowledge gap on that issue is relatively high.[2]

A high-intensity issue in community R was the question of mercury pollution in a popular lake adjoining the town. This lake had been put on a "mercury danger list" by a heavily publicized state-federal report several months before the study. A local weekly newspaper editorially claimed that the community had been treated unfairly in the report and stood to lose part of its resort business as a result. The crisis became an almost classical example of the informational consequences of an issue embodying an economic and social threat to a community. More than 98% of the respondents in community R knew about the issue, more than for any other single issue in all 19 communities. "The whole town talked" about the issue, and information distribution across educational levels was highly uniform; the knowledge gap correlation is only .04.

A similar high-conflict issue, with a resulting low knowledge gap, is in community O, where the high-voltage power line was a matter of intense concern and where opposition to the line project was organized. The correlation between knowledge and education in that community is only .06.

EVIDENCE ON THE KNOWLEDGE GAP

Theoretically, there should be a greater tendency for knowledge gaps to appear in more pluralistic communities than in more homogeneous ones. Few opportunities to test this hypothesis directly exist in view of the relative scarcity of community-level data on similar or identical issues. However, one set of data from the studies provides a partial test of the effect of community structure on the conflict dimensions of the issues and, therefore, on the magnitude of the knowledge gap. These are data from two points in time in four different communities—C, J, L, and H. In 1970 and again in 1972 in these communities, surveys were conducted to measure knowledge level on three issues   whether to mine in a wilderness area near community L, environmental restrictions on a taconite plant near community J, and closing of a steel plant at community C partly because of air pollution. Community H was a comparison center for this part of the analysis.

Media attention to the mining and steel plant issues had generally declined between 1970 and 1972, while the taconite issue remained highly controversial. However, by the time of the 1972 survey the issue had been in court once and another trial was pending. With the decline in media attention to the mining and steel plant issues, the level of current knowledge of all three topics generally declined in the four communities between the first and second surveys.

The two-year data from these communities allow for inspection of data relevant to three aspects of the knowledge gap hypothesis. One is the question of community structure: Given that community C is the most pluralistic community, will the knowledge gap on nonlocal issues be greater there than in the less pluralistic communities? A second is the question of local impact: Will the gap be lower for a given issue in the community where that issue has the most immediate local impact? A third question concerns the decline in publicity on two of the issues and a drop in familiarity: As public attention to an issue declines, will there be a corresponding drop in the knowledge gap where such gaps existed initially?

For methodological reasons, it is necessary to present these knowledge gap data in a different way. The high proportions having no knowledge of the issues in 1972 produced highly skewed distributions on this dimension which fail to meet the normality assumptions of linear correlation. Therefore, the data (Table 7-1) are presented in terms of the difference in proportion having any accurate knowledge between two different groups. These two groups are the high school and grade school groups combined and the college-educated group.

These data are generally consistent with the hypothesis based on community pluralism. On the two nonlocal issues in community C (mining and taconite), the 1970 gaps were greater

Table 7-1   Knowledge Differentials Between College-Educated
and High School or Grade School-Educated Segments,
by Community, Topic, and Year

	(4,904) Community L		(3,504) Community J		(7,247) Community H		(100,578) Community C	
Issue	1970	1972	1970	1972	1970	1972	1970	1972
Mining	+5	+7	+17	−3	+12	+9	+24	+18
Taconite	+18	+28	0	−6	+22	+16	+32	−1
Steel	+25	−4	+10	+16	+35	+18	+15	−1

NOTE: Boxes refer to the community in which that issue had the most immediate
local significance, in the sense that the question of mining pertained to an area near
Community L, the taconite plant is at Community J, and the steel plant was in
Community C itself.

The knowledge measure used in computing these differentials is based upon the
proportion in the community sample having any accurate knowledge about current
aspects of the issue. The figures in the table reflect the differential, in percentage
points, between the college group and the high school and grade school combined.
Thus, a +5 on the mining issue in Community L in 1970 indicates that the college
group was 5 percentage points higher in having any accurate knowledge on that issue
than the group with less education.

than in any one of the other three communities at a time when
the issues were most salient. Also, on the local issue, the 1970
knowledge gap in community C was greater than the corresponding gap for either of the smaller, more homogeneous communities. That is, the gap for steel knowledge in C during 1970
was greater than the gap for taconite in J or for mining in L.
Despite heavy publicity on the steel plant issue in both community C newspapers and in other media in the state, as well as
the high-conflict proportions of the issues, they showed a 15
percentage point differential between the two segments of the
population. The pluralistic nature of this metropolitan community, with its greater diversity of social concerns and economic support, seems to be a major factor.

Concerning the second question above, these data suggest
that an issue with sharp local impact, arousing general concern
about community survival and maintenance, is likely to be
accompanied by more equal distribution of knowledge. In community L, in 1970, the gap was low (5 points) for the local

mining issue and 18 and 25 points, respectively, for the taconite and steel issues. In community J, the knowledge gap for the taconite issue was zero in 1970, whereas gaps did appear for each of the other two issues.

In community H, the 1970 pattern is consistent. None of the issues had immediate local impact, and community H had a more diversified structure (though under 10,000 population) than J or L. It is nevertheless true that the impact of mining on tourism had more potential relevance to community H than did either taconite or steel; well under 20% of the respondents of that community reported occupations related in any way to steel or taconite production, lowest of all four communities. Therefore, the lower knowledge gap in community H on the mining issue in 1970, compared with greater gaps on the other two issues, is consistent with general social and economic conditions of that community.

Changes in the magnitude of the gaps from 1970 to 1972 are consistent with the basic knowledge gap hypothesis. Where gaps do exist as a result of media attention and other factors, a decline in attention to the issues from mass media and other social institutions will lead to a reduction of the gap as knowledge itself declines. Only two cases appear in Table 7-1 where gaps, if relatively high initially, did not decline in 1972. One is on the steel issue in J, where the increase is negligible. The other is the taconite issue in L. A relevant factor is that the continuing legal battle over the taconite plant remained in the news longer than the other two issues. Another factor is that in community L shortly before the 1972 study, a second weekly newspaper began publication in competition with an established one. This new weekly gave heavy attention to both the mining and taconite issues and its initial efforts to gain circulation may well have contributed to a widening knowledge gap, assuming a possible tendency for a newly established paper to be acquired first by more highly educated segments.

SUMMARY

Whenever an innovation is introduced into a social system, those segments already organized to accommodate the innovation are likely to be the first to adopt it and benefit from it. Social programs generally tend to differentially benefit those groups and individuals who have already changed or are changing in the direction of the program planners and, often, the programs contribute to a widening of any existing gap between the haves and have nots.

Knowledge about public affairs and related scientific and technical issues appears to be a specific case of the general rule: In the typical case of publicizing a topic, those who are already more knowledgeable tend to acquire the new information at a faster rate than those who are less knowledgeable. As a result, efforts of mass media and purposive communication programs designed to raise the level of knowledge throughout a community or region generally tend to increase the knowledge gap between persons with lower and higher educational levels.

The extent of the knowledge gap will vary according to other characteristics of the community and of the particular topic. A highly diverse communication system, where individuals may choose from a large array of magazines, newspapers, books, television programs, and radio stations may lead to ever-widening gaps on specialized topics. Specialization is a process of creation of groups with knowledge that increasingly sets them apart from the population generally. The more diverse and specialized the communication system becomes, the more specific will be the message content selected by individuals so as to reinforce their special interests.

Among the conditions that may lead to greater equalization of knowledge within a social system is social conflict of the type associated with community issues of basic concern to the population generally. As an issue becomes more intense, an increasing amount of newspaper publicity is generated and attention to that publicity increases. The conflict stimulates discussion among different persons, so that the joint result is a narrowing (but not necessarily an elimination) of knowledge gaps on the issue. While the evidence for these generalizations is from local and regional issues, national issues occasionally may reach such intense levels that knowledge about them tends to equalize across educational segments.

A more general question, however, is whether the types of conflicts seen at the community level in the studies reported here, and on the national level as evidenced by the Watergate issue, are representative of the processes involved in most public affairs areas. These data indicate that the knowledge gap may narrow under certain conditions of conflict intensity surrounding matters of basic concern to individuals collectively. On the other hand, the evidence indicates that in the absence of such intensity, the mechanisms for knowledge generation and distribution, including the mass media, tend to produce ever-widening gaps. The general institutionalized tendency to deal with public matters at a low-key level may then be seen as part of a larger pattern of social control that reinforces existing inequalities in information.

NOTES

1. The question of access to information was often made explicit in the power-line controversy. In one hearing concerning route designations, a power association attorney was questioning a farmer who had previously made statements at the hearing concerning costs of various forms of structures for the power line. The farmer had quoted a power association figure indicating that one type of structure would be $8 million more costly for a given stretch of line. The attorney asked "Do you have reason to expect that figure is right?" The farmer answered: "That's the problem. There are no sources of information we can use unless *you* supply it."

2. Community R provides still another illustration of how local relevance of an issue can be related to intensity of conflict. The nuclear power plant, being located in a different county, was not a matter of intense concern when the study was conducted in community R in 1971. Another energy issue, however (the power line), was an extremely volatile issue in that community in later years. In 1977 and 1978, some of the most intense, highly organized, and potentially violent encounters of Minnesota's power-line struggle occurred in the county of which community R is the county seat. The power line had first been considered for one part of the county, but the area was shifted as a result of the corridor hearings when an organized group of irrigation farmers made strong objections. The new location was in another part of the county, across other farm land, and for a time opposition leaders included persons in both sections of the county.

REFERENCES

ARNOVE, R. F. (1975) "Sociopolitical implications of educational television." Journal of Communication 25: 144-156.

BOGART, L. (1975) "How the challenge of television news affects the prosperity of daily newspapers." Journalism Quarterly 52: 403-410.

CHAFFEE, S. H. and L. B. BECKER (1975) "Young voters' reactions to early Watergate issues." American Politics Quarterly 3: 360-385.

CHU, G. (1968) "Impact of mass media on a Gemeinschaft-like social structure." Rural Sociology 33: 189-199.

CUMMINGS, S., R. BRIGGS, and J. MERCY (1977) "Preachers vs. teachers: local-cosmopolitan conflict over textbook censorship in an Appalachian community." Rural Sociology 42: 7-21.

DAVIS, R. C. (1958) The Public Impact of Science in the Mass Media. Ann Arbor: University of Michigan Institute for Social Research.

DeFLEUR, M. (1966) Theories of Mass Communication. New York: David McKay.

DONOHUE, G. A., P. J. TICHENOR, and C. N. OLIEN (1975) "Mass media and the knowledge gap: a hypothesis reconsidered." Communication Research 2: 3-23.

FUNKHOUSER, G. R. and N. MACCOBY (1973) "Tailoring science writing to the general audience." Journalism Quarterly 50: 220-226.

GERBNER, G. and L. GROSS (1976) "Living with television: the violence profile." Journal of Communication 26: 173-199.

HAGSTROM, W. (1965) The Scientific Community. New York: Basic Books.

JOHNSTONE, J.W.C. (1965) Volunteers for Learning. Chicago: AVC.

LYND, R. and H. M. LYND (1929) Middletown: A Study in Contemporary American Culture. New York: Harcourt Brace Jovanovich.

MANDELBAUM, S. (1972) Community and Communications. New York: Norton.

McLUHAN, M. (1964) Understanding Media: The Extension of Man. New York: McGraw-Hill.

McNELLY, J. (1973) "Mass media and information redistribution." Environmental Education 5: 31-64.

MERTON, R. (1972) "Insiders and outsiders: a chapter in the sociology of knowledge." American Journal of Sociology 78: 9-47.

NEUMAN, W. R. (1976) "The patterns of recall among television news viewers." Public Opinion Quarterly 40: 115-123.

RAINWATER, L. (1969) "The problem of lower-class culture and poverty-war strategy," pp. 229-259 in D. P. Moynihan (ed.) On Understanding Poverty. New York: Basic Books.

ROBINSON, J. (1967) "World affairs information and mass media exposure." Journalism Quarterly 44: 23-31.

ROGERS, E. M. (1976) "Communication and development: the passing of the dominant paradigm." Communication Research 3: 213-240.

ROLIG, N. G., J. ASCROFT, and F. WaCHEGE (1976) "The diffusion of innovations and the issue of equity in rural development." Communication Research 3: 155-169.

SAMUELSON, M., R. CARTER, and L. RUGGELS (1963) "Education, available time and use of mass media." Journalism Quarterly 40: 491-496.

SCHRAMM, W. and S. WADE (1967) Knowledge and the Public Mind. Palo Alto, CA: Stanford University Institute for Communication Research.

SHINGI, P. M. and B. MODY (1976) "The communications effects gap: a field experiment on television and agricultural ignorance in India." Communication Research 3: 171-190.

SIGAL, L. (1973) Reporters and Officials: The Organization and Politics of Newsmaking. Lexington, MA: D. C. Heath.

STAR, S. A. and H. M. HUGHES (1950) "Report on an educational campaign: the Cincinnati Plan for the United Nations." American Journal of Sociology 55: 389-400.

SUOMINEN, E. (1976) "Who needs information and why." Journal of Communication 26: 115-119.

TICHENOR, P. J., G. A. DONOHUE, and C. N. OLIEN (1970) "Mass media flow and differential growth in knowledge." Public Opinion Quarterly 34: 159-170.

WARREN, R. (1973) "The sociology of knowledge and the problems of the inner cities," pp. 321-339 in R. Warren (ed.) Perspectives on the American Community. Skokie, IL: Rand-McNally.

WERNER, A. (1975) "A case of sex and class socialization." Journal of Communication 25: 45-50.

WESTLEY, B. and W. SEVERIN (1963) "How Wisconsinites use and appraise their daily newspapers and other media." University of Wisconsin School of Journalism. (mimeo)

8

Knowledge, Education,
and
Support for
Courses of Action

Among the favored beliefs about public information is the idea that increasing the level of citizen knowledge about a new proposal will lead to a change in citizen points of view about that proposal. It is not unusual, for example, to hear advocates of a new facility, such as an electric generating plant, contend that "if people learn the facts" about the problem, more public support for the generating plant will follow. Proponents of various action programs often say that "people have to be educated to understand" the need for a project.

Available evidence supports the conclusion that increasing the level of knowledge about a proposal leads to a systematic change in opinions about it only when certain conditions prevail. One situation that might lead to increased support for a project, as citizen knowledge increases, is domination of the channels by groups advocating a particular point of view, with no open debate or challenge. Such a condition assumes that the community is structured in such a fashion as to permit rather monolithic presentation of an argument or that the issue is of such a nature that it does not have differential benefits for various groups. Hence, the issue does not contain the necessary ingredients for conflict development. Mendelsohn (1973) noted several cases in which opinions on health and safety subjects were modified following information campaigns that raised citizen levels of knowledge about these topics. In a recent community experiment, Maccoby and Farquhar (1975) demonstrated changes not only in opinions but also in behavior and blood lipid levels as well, following a media information campaign on health and behavior practices related to heart disease. Typically, these studies, such as the one by Maccoby and Farquhar, occur in situations where there are few if any counterarguments about the experimental topic in the mass media.

Where there is a contest between alternative points of view, however, it is unlikely that a higher level of knowledge by itself will necessarily lead to formation of one set of opinions or another. When different groups within the structure present conflicting arguments, the information and interpretations of its implication for courses of action may become central to the debate, as pointed out by Marceau (1972) and as discussed here in previous chapters.

When intense debates occur, as they did in the power-line issue, the conflict process produces a situation in which being highly informed is being aware of differential group interests and differential positions on the issue. In the case of fluoridation, increased levels of knowledge among citizens often did not lead to greater support for the idea (Crain, Katz, and Rosenthal, 1969). However, open support for fluoridation by mayors and newspaper editorials often was associated with support for that course of action among citizens, a finding which is consistent with the interpretation that one-sided organization in a community is more likely to lead to community acceptance of a predetermined outcome.

CONFLICT AND OPINIONS ABOUT COURSES OF ACTION

Data from 12 Minnesota communities make it possible to make a preliminary test about the implications of varying degrees of community conflict for the relationship between citizen support of a particular course of action and levels of knowledge about the issue.

The hypothesis is that within communities where there are higher degrees of conflict intensity, lower correlations exist between citizen level of knowledge about an issue and support of a particular course of action. A corresponding hypothesis is that within communities where conflict intensity is higher, there will be lower correlations between citizen level of education and support for a particular course of action.

These hypotheses are based on the assumption that typically, when there is little controversy about a subject in a community, knowledge is confined largely to those individuals whose community roles tend to require a degree of familiarity with the subject and a perspective about it. Generally, these are participant roles and are more likely to occur in the highly educated stratum of the community. Perspectives held when there is an absence of competition among various interest groups are characteristic of the status position of these roles and reflect the collective self-interest of this segment of the community. More highly educated persons, for example, tend to have above average levels of knowledge about community affairs generally and may tend in the absence of conflict to favor such community improvement projects as new schools, urban development, new sewage facilities, and new hospitals.

However, support for community projects may not be based on general values of a given stratum when there is a community controversy about those projects. Whereas in the absence of controversy, highly educated persons may be especially supportive of strong restrictions on industrial pollution, they may be less supportive of those controls in a controversy. If organizational and communication efforts of countervailing groups are successful, the more highly informed and highly educated segments of the community are likely to divide on the issue according to specific group interests rather than values more generally characteristic of their socioeconomic level.

Assume there is a local debate over placing environmental restrictions on an industry, restrictions which are seen by some groups as damaging to both that industry's future and the survival of the community. In such a debate, a conflict leads to more effective organization, which in turn leads to greater sensitivity and learning because of vested interests. When different groups present differing views on this issue, they generally seek leaders who are seen as credible and informed, and their statements are geared to appeal to the highly educated. Studies of the fluoridation debates indicate that leaders of opposition as well as proponent groups tended to be relatively well educated and to occupy participant roles in public affairs. Similarly, leaders of the opposition to nuclear power plants also were found to be above average in education, with 73% having at least a bachelor's degree (Mazur, 1975).

DATA FROM COMMUNITIES

Three groups of community studies in the project make it possible to examine relationships among level of knowledge, levels of education, and support for courses of action. These are the political regionalization issue, the mining and metal industries issue, and the power-line issue. In each group, the same issue was involved in four communities and identical measures of support for a particular course of action were used. In the political regionalization issue, the scale is a measure of the extent to which persons favor the regional development concept. In the power-line study, the measure is based on a single item asking whether the respondent agrees or disagrees that the high-voltage transmission line "should be built in this county wherever the electric power association says is best." In the mining and metal industries study group, the first surveys conducted in 1970 included indentical questions in four communities about whether respondents supported the idea of mining in the Boundary Waters Canoe Area. The measure of knowledge is the one used in previous analyses in this report, the number of accurate statements which respondents made in response to an open-end item asking what he or she had "seen or heard" recently about the topic.

There was a fourth community group in which it is possible to examine the relationship between education and attitudes toward water quality, but not about knowledge concerning water quality since somewhat different local issues were involved. The attitude scale measured the extent to which persons favor an environmentalist position on sewage control and protection of water in rivers and lakes.

OPINIONS AND KNOWLEDGE

The data provide partial support for the hypothesis that within communities where there are higher degrees of conflict intensity, lower correlations are found between citizen level of knowledge about an issue and support of a particular course of action concerning that issue. In the mining and metal industries study, the lowest correlation between level of knowledge and support for mining (.06) was in community L, where the highest percentage of respondents (51%) perceived the issue as controversial (Figure 8-1). However, the *second* lowest correlation is in community J, where the *lowest* degree of conflict is perceived, and the correlations are highest in the two communities which are intermediate on perception of conflict. A very similar curvilinear pattern appears on the power-line issue where, again, the community with the highest perception of conflict (community O) has the lowest correlation between knowledge about the issue and opposition to the building of the line, while the second lowest correlation is in the community with the lowest degree of perceived conflict. Therefore, the data from these two study groups support the hypothesis only to the extent that in each case, the community with the highest level of conflict has the weakest link between level of knowledge and support for a particular course of action. In each case, where a correlation did occur, it meant that the higher the knowledge, the more support for a course of action consistent with a community self-interest point of view.

In the case of the political regionalization study group, the results do not support the hypothesis that in communities with

Figure 8.1   Percent Perceiving Conflict in Issue and
Correlation Between Knowledge and Opinions

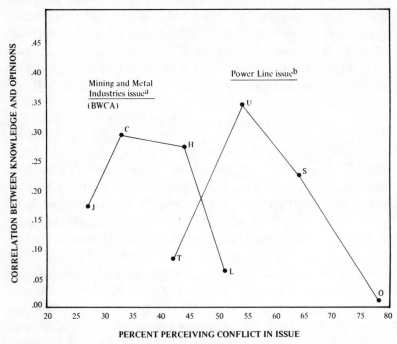

a. Opinion scale is scored so that a positive correlation means that the higher the
    knowledge, the greater the support for the environmentalist position on the
    BWCA issue. "Perceived conflict" in this group is based on response to open-
    end item.

b. A single opinion item is used, scored so that a positive correlation means the
    higher the knowledge, the greater the disagreement that "New high voltage
    transmission lines should be built wherever the electric power association says
    is best." Perceived conflict is based on percent saying issue is a "touchy subject."

higher levels of conflict, weaker correlations appear between
level of knowledge and support for a course of action. In that
case, the lowest correlation between level of knowledge about
regional development and support for the regional development
concept (r = .001) was in community G where the subject was
least controversial. In the other three communities, the correlations were stronger, but *different* in sign. In community I, the
correlation was -.36; in community B, which had the highest
level of conflict, the correlation was -.17; and in community A

it was +.16. The issue was perceived as relatively low in conflict in all communities; only in community B did more than 20% perceive regional development as a touchy subject. Wide differences in correlations between the level of knowledge and support for the concept may reflect the nature of the issue was quite different among these communities, with different arguments relevant to the topic in each one. In community B, the regional development plan had been attacked by the local daily newspaper as misguided and unfair to area communities. Yet, the four communities varied little on overall opinions about the issue. The reaction toward regional development was slightly more negative in community B (where the newspaper challenge had occurred) than in the other three, but the differences were not sharp; 73% in community B agreed that "local governments everywhere in Minnesota ought to join together for regional planning and government." That compares with 81%, 77%, and 76% agreeing in communities A, I, and G, respectively.

These data are consistent in indicating that high levels of knowledge do not necessarily accompany a particular type of opinion, in either conflictive or nonconflictive situations. Several kinds of community situations result in only a weak relationship (if any at all) between level of knowledge and support for a particular course of action on an issue. These findings, along with others from previous studies, do not support the contention that raising the level of knowledge about issues would lead to a particular modification of attitudes for or against a particular project, proposal, or decision. These findings also provide tentative support for the hypothesis that when conflict reaches an extremely high level, the link between level of knowledge and support for a course of action tends to be especially weak.

LEVEL OF EDUCATION AND OPINIONS

The data present stronger evidence for the hypothesis that within communities where there are higher degrees of conflict intensity, there will be lower correlations between citizen level of education and support for a particular course of action (Figures 8-2 and 8-3). In the case of the political regionalization issue, the correlation between level of education and support for the regional development concept declines as conflict increases. Similarly, in the case of water quality, level of education is more closely tied to an environmentalist position on sewage control and water quality protection in community E, where the issue of sewage control was seen as least controversial among the four communities.

In the power-line issue (Figure 8-2), one community diverges rather sharply from the monotonic pattern characteristic of the other two issues. This is community S, which is high on perception of conflict and also has as high a correlation between education and opposition to the power line as does the community with the lowest conflict level. No readily available explanation is offered for this departure. It is not necessarily a case of high perceived self-interest among the highly educated, since the correlation between level of education and perception of "direct effect" of the line on the respondent in community S was low (r = .10).

Similarly, the mining and metal industries issue (Figure 8-3) offers general support for the hypothesis, with one community standing apart. That is community H, in which next to highest conflict is perceived, along with a relatively high correlation between level of education and support for mining. Community H is geographically most distant from the area to which the "support-for-mining" items referred, so that the perceived conflict in this case is not necessarily a local one.

CONFLICT AND PREDICTABILITY OF OPINIONS

The foregoing data are consistent in one important respect. Where local conflict is perceived as most intense, support for a given course of action shows the weakest correlation with both level of knowledge and level of education. Other conditions may produce such weak linkages, particularly where level of knowledge is concerned, but a highly intense controversy at the

Figure 8.2   Perception on "Touchiness" and Correlation
Between Education and Opinions in 12 Communities

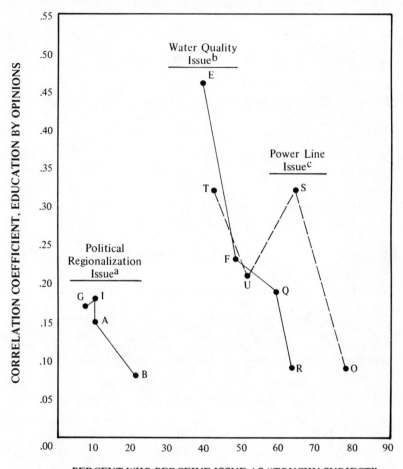

a. Scale, scored so that a positive correlation means that the higher the education, the greater the support for the regional development concept.

b. Scale, scored so that a positive correlation means that the higher the education, the greater the support for a pro-environmentalist position on sewage control and protection of water in rivers and lakes.

c. A single item, scored so that a positive correlation means that the higher the education, the greater the opposition to placing the line "wherever the power associations say is best."

Figure 8.3   Perception of Conflict and Correlation
Between Education and Opinions about Environmental
Restrictions on the BWCA in Four Communities, 1970[a]

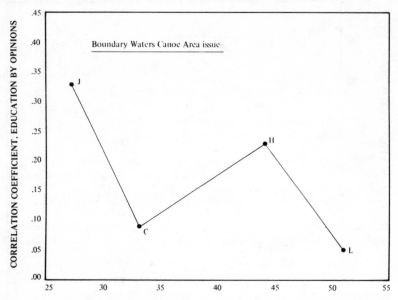

PERCENT PERCEIVING CONFLICT IN ISSUE, BASED ON OPEN-END QUESTION

a. Opinion scale is scored so that a positive correlation means that the higher the
    education, the greater the support for the environmentalist position on the
    BWCA (canoe country) issue.

local level appears to reduce the likelihood that points of view
can be predicted either from what persons know or from their
educational status. One consequence of high levels of conflict
intensity may be greater awareness of varying and conflicting
points of view among more and less educated persons alike. One
might expect a relatively strong relationship between level of
education and support for action when an issue is introduced to
the public and a decline in that relationship as the issue becomes the focal point of conflict among competing interest
groups. The more a conflict develops, the more the highly
educated groups in the community may take varying sides and
the more likely all sides will be to present information that their
adherents will acquire and remember. Information and highly

trained persons are fundamental resources in a conflict, and it is theoretically reasonable to expect a contest for both.

REFERENCES

CRAIN, R. L., E. KATZ, and D. B. ROSENTHAL (1969) The Politics of Community Conflict: The Fluoridation Decision. Indianapolis: Bobbs-Merrill.

HOVLAND, C. I., I. L. JANIS, and H. H. KELLEY (1953) Communication and Persuasion: Psychological Studies of Opinion Change. New Haven, CT: Yale University Press.

MACCOBY, N. and J. FARQUHAR (1975) "Communication for health: unselling heart disease." Journal of Communication 25: 114-126.

MARCEAU, F. J. (1972) "Communication and development: a reconsideration." Public Opinion Quarterly 36: 235-245.

MAZUR, A. (1975) "Opposition to technological innovation." Minerva 13 (spring): 58-81.

MENDELSOHN, H. (1973) "Some reasons why information campaigns can succeed." Public Opinion Quarterly 37: 50-61.

9

Summary

The analysis of conflict situations provides abundant evidence that newspapers and other media of communication are not the independent, self-styled social agents that either they or members of the public may imagine them to be. The efficacy of viewing the press, or any other mass medium, as constituting a separate "fourth estate" is doubtful at best. The press is an integral subsystem within the total system, and its strong linkages with other system components impinge upon it as much as it impinges upon them, if not more.

Structural constraints on the press may be partly obscured by a traditional tendency to view newspapers as creations of individuals and, therefore, as extensions of their personalities. Legendary accounts of Pulitzer, Ochs, McCormick, the Hearsts, and other major figures in journalism appear to have contributed to this view. From a structural perspective, however, the emergence of Colonel McCormick and the Chicago *Tribune* should be understood in the context of Chicago as a particular type of developing metropolis at a particular point in time. In this perspective, newspapers constitute a media subsystem with structurally defined roles which give rise to "media magnates," who have been largely submerged by current media corporate powers.

Structural constraints can be illustrated by what may and may not occur when a new publisher, or an out-of-town newspaper chain, buys the local newspaper and shortly thereafter changes its size, type face, and writing style. This supposedly new newspaper—with even its name now appearing in modern, clean-edged type rather than in the familiar antique type face used for the previous 57 years—may seem to some observers as a work of individual creative art. Or some may see it as an individual blunder. But if one considers the community circumstances, one typically will find that graphic changes are often related largely to technological changes growing out of changes in the organization of newspaper production. In newspaper *content,* the new owner is severely limited in the scope of changes which can be made.

He or she will find the same agencies, business groups, citizen organizations, and other power centers that existed previously, all of them having institutionalized arrangements with the paper and expectations about what the newspaper will report and how it will report it. There will be corresponding expectations about the role of the editor in the community, what his or her relationships will be with other groups, what information that editor may receive and provide for others, and what the standards will be for judging that editor's performance. These expectations within the structure determine what in fact constitutes "all the news that's fit to print."

These arrangements and expectations do not yield easily to drastic change. If the school superintendent, county extension agents, social welfare director, and two ministers have been contributing news and commentary columns to the paper on a regular basis, those columns will not be dropped without major repercussions for editor-community relations. If there has been a regularized pattern of coverage of city council meetings, in which reporters cover some meetings and not others, and make routine and frequent contacts with certain council members and city agency heads, this pattern will tend to be imposed on new reporters and editors, as many a journalist new to a given community has learned.[1] If the local hospital and county medical society have developed an informal but rigidly observed division of responsibility for public reporting of certain kinds of health and medical news, a new editor will find these arrangements difficult if not impossible to overturn. And if the editor decides to eliminate a "theatre critique" column in favor of more space on local movies and television programming, the editor may well face a delegation from the community actors' organization wondering why the newspaper has given up this "vital aspect of community service."[2]

This is not to say that change cannot and will not occur in the community press, but that it will tend to be gradual and done in a way that is largely determined by, and easy to accommodate within, the community structure. Changes in type face, layout, and photographic coverage are relatively easy to justify as improvements in journalistic quality and as necessary for economic reasons. Offset printing *was* generally adopted earlier by small-town weekly papers than by larger, urban daily papers, owing partly to the fact that the flat-bed press technology of the weeklies had been antiquated even before obsolescence overcame the more specialized rotary letter press of the daily newspaper publishing industry. What is important to note about this change is that while it led to greater economies in publishing and modernization in appearance of newspapers, it does not appear to have produced substantial change in content of newspapers or their relationships to their communities. From a structural standpoint, one would expect such changes to be accommodated within the system with minimal consequences for basic social relations, even though it may have appreciable structural effects for such specific groups as press and linotype operators whose livelihood and stature were tied to the outdated technology.

As an integral part of the community, the newspaper reflects the concerns of the dominant power groupings. The term *reflects* is appropriate in the sense that it is neither a total nor an undistorted reproduction of current events and institutions.

Newspapers reflect selectively, in ways determined not by editorial idiosyncrasy but by the structure and distribution of social power in the community. A newspaper in a one-industry town is unlikely to report that industry in a critical way. It will reflect community consensus about that industry through reporting socially noncontroversial aspects of that industry and generally avoiding reports that would question it.

ROLE OF THE PRESS IN CONFLICT

While the press does serve as a mirror, however contorted its reflective curvature, it is part of a reciprocal process, being affected *by* that system and affecting it in turn. Rather than being an initiator of basic positions, the press is normally pushed into reporting events by organized forces in the system and its reports become an integral part of the social process which bear on the nature of future events. Community groups may use the press and journalists as sources of intelligence, as indications of reaction of the public to events, and as a device for creating awareness and defining problems. The performance of the press or other medium typically becomes part of the controversy.

The Watergate episode is frequently cited as an example of how the press creates an issue. Yet Watergate indicates the basic nature of the linkages between the press and other components of society, including the legal and political structures and the interest groups that exist in every issue. An indication of this linkage is the fact that throughout the 1972 election campaign, neither the Washington *Post* nor Senator McGovern succeeded in making the Watergate issue a dominant national concern. Not until the problem was defined so as to involve a significant attack on the entire social structure (i.e., democracy) did it become an issue of national concern.

As is evident to the reader of the preceding chapters, the general frame of reference of this work emphasizes the structural conditions which set the parameters for behavior of both the subsystems and the personalities participating in those systems. Just as "no man is an island," subsystems are integrated into larger systems. The press is no exception, and the generalizations presented below are illustrative of this perspective.

NEWSPAPERS AND INFORMATION CONTROL

One generalization is that information is part of a general process of social control which includes media participation within different social structures. Information is a prime resource in the creation and maintenance of social power, a point which may become increasingly visible as social conflicts progress. Importance of information control is illustrated by the increasing development of specialized communication centers in business, government, education, and other agencies and interest groups. It is a rare collective action group that does not develop an organizational role or set of roles in communication, carrying titles such as public relations, publicity, outreach, or even "communication specialist." Public dissemination of information may be concentrated in the top leadership of an organization, particularly in the early stages of organization, with communication specialties added as the group grows and becomes increasingly bureaucratized.

These communication roles deal continually with questions of whether to transmit something, how to transmit it, and who the audience will be. Tensions over communications may be among the most common strains, if not *the* most common, within most organizations. Even though there may be a widespread belief that disagreements and conflicts are undesirable, creation of communication roles does not necessarily lessen the intensity of conflicts.

COMMUNITY STRUCTURE, MEDIA, AND MEDIA USE

A second generalization is that since communication subsystems are themselves creations of the larger structures in which they operate, both media personnel performance and media use patterns of citizens will differ according to structural characteristics.

In a more highly specialized and diverse urban structure, the reporter is more likely to have a relationship with sources that are limited to the news gathering function, compared with a reporter in the more homogeneous small-town structure. As a consequence, the urban reporter is more autonomous within the system as a whole, vis-à-vis the sources, since the more pluralistic structure tends to reinforce separation of roles according to professional specialization and relationships. This separation may be illustrated by the legal profession. Lawyers may engage their professional capacities in what may appear to be sharp, if not acrimonious debate, in the court room. An hour later, the same lawyers may have a good-humored discussion over coffee about another topic entirely. By contrast, the small-town journalist is more likely to have a multiplicity of interactions with sources, knowing them as citizens, members of social clubs, and/or as members of friendship groups in settings that make it difficult if not impossible to separate the professional from the purely social or personal relationship. The urban lawyers are better able to isolate their courtroom encounters from their chats over coffee because the structure in which they operate encourages such differentiation.

Similarly, media use patterns differ according to community structure. In a small, more tradition-oriented rural community, the local weekly newspaper tends to be dominated by local news, and citizens are less likely to read daily newspapers than are citizens of larger urban centers served by dailies. Without the diverse combination of local, state, and national news that urban citizens get in their daily newspapers, residents of small communities can choose between distant urban dailies and broadcast media for news about the larger society. Television, with its particular combination of visual and audio appeal, becomes more strongly preferred for nonlocal news in the small town and rural area than is true in the urban center. McLuhan (1964) contended that the "medium is the message"; we would modify that by stating that the "structure is the message," since the structural parameters determine what the media will be and, to a considerable degree, what media use patterns will develop.

These differential media uses lead to different combinations of use patterns that organized groups must take into account if they are to reach the larger public through the various channels that exist. The question of how interest groups develop strategies for different community and media structures is a fruitful area for further study. These strategies require far more than analyzing the audience, finding the media that achieve high audience attention, and placing messages in those media. The "media event" techniques, such as demonstrations or whatever form they take, often involve the media personnel in such a way that they lead to quite different content than might occur if a press release were simply "placed" through routine editorial handling of purposive communications. Reporter involvement in reporting a media event does not necessarily mean the reporter thereby will be sympathetic to the organization staging the event, even though the possibility exists for such sympathy to develop. What is crucial for the strategy of countervailing groups, typically, is that the event be covered and given prominent display by the media. Reports of demonstrations, confrontations, and other media events in a newspaper may gain a level of public awareness and salience which a press release from one side alone is unlikely to have. Journalists may even be hostile to the group staging the event, but it is possible for media reports to bestow *greater* saliency on the issue as a result. McLuhan (1964) makes a similar point in discussing the Nazi party's rise to prominence in Germany in the 1920s and early 1930s, even with mass media that were not sympathetic to the organization. American presidents, such as Franklin Roosevelt, may well have *benefited* from press opposition which led both to attention to his candidacy and to his challenges to elite groups which the newspapers, as business firms, symbolize.

SYSTEM REINFORCEMENT OF THE MEDIA ROLE

A third generalization is that since they are dependent upon other parts of the system, newspapers and other media participate in social conflict in circumscribed ways which are reinforced within the system. Media will tend to reflect the perspectives of organizational power centers, which is apparent not only in small, homogeneous communities but is also illuminated in communities or regions where values and outlooks on major issues are highly diverse. Where there is diversity in social power, media tend to reflect the orientations of those segments that are higher on the power scale. In the American experience, this means having the general outlook of the business community, as a number of observers have pointed out (Hennessy, 1976; Davis, Bredemeier, and Levy, 1949; Breed, 1958).

This tendency to reflect the outlook of business and other dominant power groups can have consequences in conflict situations which, while not always immediately apparent to participants in a struggle, are quite understandable within a structural framework. In the power-line episode, as indicated in earlier chapters, the weekly newspapers in the rural communities generally reported the issue in ways reinforcing the conclusion that the whole town was united in opposition to the line. However, there *were* divisions of views on these issues in those communities, with local business groups often taking no specific stand on the power line. It is also true that during the initial corridor hearings and route designation hearings, views of these business groups were rarely reported in the press, except in a few cases where certain business groups did speak against the line being built where interests of those groups might have been adversely affected. Otherwise, business groups were not widely quoted on the controversy.

From the local business point of view, the power-line controversy contained two quite separate issues. On the question of outside interference in community decisions, one would expect the business groups to be generally sympathetic with the protesters. On the more general question of power utilities, one would expect the local business groups to be generally favorable, as they would toward any commercial development that might enhance the local business climate.

In this setting, the general nonmention of the business point of view by newspapers in early stages of the power-line conflict should not be interpreted as *divergence* from that view. On the contrary, the same structural factors which in the absence of countervailing group organization would lead to newspaper reporting of establishment perspectives appear to have contributed to the avoiding of news reports of direct challenges of those perspectives during the struggle. With views of local business and political groups thus unchallenged, there was little inconsistency in the papers' reverting to actively reporting such views as the confrontations diminished and construction of the line proceeded.

Following the period of field confrontation, newspaper coverage given the issue concentrated on reports of vandalism, acts of violence against power-line employees, and of damage to power-line towers and other property. Such reporting no longer gave an impression of solidarity in local opposition to the line. One newspaper, whose earlier reports had emphasized local opposition, in later stages reprinted an editorial from another newspaper that referred to the protesters' battle as lost and futile, concluding that "it's time that protesting farmers stop hindering progress of power line survey crews" and that "there is little question" of a need for the electricity.

Structurally, it is predictable that media reports will tend to "back the winner," that is, to reflect the locus of social power and to be reinforced within the system for doing so. The protest groups were beaten, the construction was obvious, and the newspapers fell in line. It would be structurally unreasonable to expect any mass medium serving a community as a whole to continue backing, through editorials or portrayals, what has come to be known as a lost cause.

This case of powerful business groups having views that may depart in some respects from those of a popular protest, even in a small community, illustrates another aspect of the theme of system reinforcement of media that one might overlook. In data gathered concerning the use of expert information, it appeared that community publics and their leaders may be marching to the beat of different drums. This difference appeared most sharply in the small communities, where leadership groups must deal both with immediate local concerns and with the link between the local community and the larger society. Just as Vidich and Bensman (1958) and Martindale and Hanson (1969) found leaders of small towns oriented toward power centers of distant urban centers as well as toward local concerns, the leaders studied here faced similarly complex sets of circumstances. The data dealt with leaders' views of the usefulness of scientific information in decision making, with small-town leaders being more favorable toward such information than their local publics. In the power-line study, a similar difference might well have been expected. That is, the power-line issue was eventually decided in hearings and court proceedings in favor of building the line, and local business and government leaders are the ones most able from their own positions in the structure to have predicted accurately that such would be the case. To them it was quite clear that the decisions would be made in favor of new sources of electricity and according to the principle of eminent domain.

Findings and illustrations here emphasize the marginal nature of leadership in the local community, and it is important to note that it is therefore a set of socially marginal power groups that constrain and reinforce communications media in their reporting of local events. Evidence available indicates that in the final analysis, many local leadership groups in the communities affected by the power line supported the outcome that was controlled by the established procedures and forces, even though that outcome was unpopular. Several newspapers, whose earlier reporting had been itself a response to the strength of the organized countervailing groups, ended up also reinforcing that outcome. The entire struggle reflects the limited power of citizen groups that oppose established forces and procedures. Within the local community, it is the power elite that ultimately shapes the media outlook and which therefore receives reciprocal reinforcement *from* those media.

INFORMATION AND CONFLICT

A fourth generalization considers knowledge as a power resource and conflict as an aspect of the process that coalesces the generation, distribution, and acquisition of knowledge. This generalization runs counter to the view that conflict produces mostly confusion, rumor, and social disorder, a view based on the belief that "emotional" issues lead to "irrationality" with "nobody listening to reason." While it is true that a wide range of intense emotions on the individual level may be aroused and expressed in a conflict, and while break-offs in communication may occur among individuals and groups, the conflict process generally creates greater need for communication at various levels and tends to increase the distribution and acquisition of knowledge among different interest groups. To oppose the power line, the protest groups needed effective arguments and concentrated initially on getting information on the questions of safety and health. To buttress their position, they located and publicly cited certain research reports dealing with safety and health aspects of high-voltage power-line installations. On the other hand, the power associations brought forth their consultants who reported research data, in far greater quantities than the protest groups had been able to muster, that they interpreted as refuting the argument that power lines were potentially unsafe.

The type of information generated and distributed tends to vary according to the needs of different groups within the structure at different stages of the conflict. In the case of the power line, emphasis upon technical questions of safety and health in the early phase was largely a result of the occurrence of a series of hearings required by state law for selection of a 20-mile-wide corridor within which the line would be located. These hearings were structured so as to concentrate not on whether the line would be built, but where. Such a hearing process ruled out consideration of the larger issue of the fairness of eminent domain proceedings and led instead toward emphasis upon technical information, bearing on the question of locating the line in one agricultural area versus another. Press coverage of the issue during this period emphasized this technical information and related research evidence, which were generated by the various interested groups to support their positions within this adversary hearing process, which constitutes a conflict accommodation mechanism.

When the conflict shifted from the state-required hearing process to field confrontations between the protesters and line construction crews, these confrontations and demonstrations became the story and the question of health and safety, while not ignored, received proportionally less attention. In this later phase of field confrontation strategies (conceived of as a "wildcat" procedure), the countervailing groups devoted proportionally more of their resources to these immediate events rather than to developing new technical arguments and producing evidence to support them. Since the hearings had failed to resolve the issue, the conflict shifted to different accommodation mechanisms that exist within the system (i.e., organized protest demonstrations) for development of innovative strategies to get a "hearing de novo" with the public at large. To do this requires the coalescing of power groups so as to organize their resources and talent for advancement of their cause under the current circumstances. In the power-line confrontations, the positions chosen during the confrontation centered on the question of fairness of the hearing procedure and, eventually, on fairness of eminent domain itself, with technical questions becoming secondary.

A perspective in general education holds that in reporting such confrontations, reporters and editors "aren't doing their job" unless they devote large amounts of space to "background" reports based on evidence from scientists and technologists. Such a perspective, however, fails to take into account the nature of the conflict process and the structural principle that editors and reporters at all stages are dependent upon the acts and statements of the various interest groups. From a structural standpoint, it is very understandable why reporters *do* become immersed in the day-to-day chronology of conflict events rather than in background analyses when the conflict reaches a phase of organized confrontations and demonstrations. For example, in the winter of 1978, during a period of intense picketing at power-line construction sites, the

Minnesota Department of Health issued a report that sum-
marized, in voluminous detail, bodies of data on health and
safety aspects of power lines. Very few newspaper stories on
this report appeared in Minnesota newspapers in succeeding
weeks, and those that did concentrated mostly on the conclusion that few dangers of such lines had been demonstrated.
Virtually none of the news articles went beyond the body of
the state's report. The consequence was to reinforce the conclusion that the opposition had no conclusive evidence for
objecting to the line on grounds of safety and, in effect, to
discourage reporters from proceeding in their search for material.

CONFLICT AND THE KNOWLEDGE GAP

A fifth generalization from this analysis is that through being
an integral part of a conflict process within a social structure,
mass media in performing their particular roles may contribute
to either the widening or narrowing of disparities in knowledge
within the system. Whether the consequence is to widen knowledge gaps or not depends at least partially upon the nature of
conflict itself. Conflict is rooted in social differentiation, and
newspapers and other media may contribute to increasing intensity and broadening of the scope of these conflicts while performing according to their traditional roles. This participation
may serve to reinforce the differences in orientations and outlooks between different interest groups and sectors of society.
While the belief is often held that modernization brings a
leveling of attitudinal differences between rural and urban areas,
much evidence including that reported here does not support
that conclusion. Debates over such issues as placing environmental restrictions on use of the Boundary Waters Canoe Area,
or on operation of a taconite processing plant in a community
depending on that plant for 80% of its employment, tend to
highlight the differences between small-town, rural areas and
those of urban areas, primarily because of the difference between homogeneous and pluralistic structures. Interest groups

advocating environmental protection are characterized by a high percentage of membership which is urban in origin and values, and their promotion of restricted use of forest and lake land is often viewed by local groups as merely a big-city desire for unspoiled vacation playgrounds.

Several studies in the social science literature reinforce the conclusion that knowledge is differentially distributed in a manner similar to other resources, meaning that it is utilized to support specific points of view of organized interest groups. Whenever an innovation or resource becomes initially available in a social system, some segments will be organized to accommodate and utilize that innovation or resource and will be the first to adopt it and reap benefits from it. This tendency has been noted with adult education programs (Johnstone, 1965), extension programs in agricultural areas (Rolig, Ascroft, and WaChege, 1976; Shingi and Mody, 1976), programs for education of disadvantaged children through television (Bogaty and Ball, 1971), and distribution of knowledge about public affairs (Wade and Schramm, 1969; Robinson, 1967). Efforts of mass media to raise knowledge levels also tend frequently to increase the knowledge gap between persons with lower and higher educational levels (Tichenor, Olien, and Donohue, 1970; Donohue, Olien, and Tichenor, 1975).

The finding of increasing knowledge gaps in a variety of situations does not mean, however, that the gaps will *always* increase. There are conditions that may lead to a decrease in gaps and to greater equalization of knowledge within a social system. One of these conditions is the existence of increasingly intense levels of social conflict, particularly that associated with community issues that touch basic concerns of different groups among the population. Conflict not only results in generation and dissemination of new knowledge but it is also an intervening variable in coalescing the concern of participating groups to acquire that knowledge. Conflict increases the amount of interaction at various points within the system and leads to a sharpening of the definition of group interests and to greater clarification in the definition of social problems. In this process, conflict leads to clarification of values of groups vis-à-vis other groups in the system and to a sharpening of each group's position. Effective group positions in social controversies include articulation of the relevance of the issue to the interests of other groups. A basic conflict strategy is to engage groups in the larger public which may have previously seen the issue as a distant fray over "somebody else's problem." A small group of employees in a container factory may conduct a strike which is not recognized by any union and may receive the "wildcat" label in newspaper headlines and broadcast news reports. The strikers' organization might then set up a media event, such as a demonstration or press conference, in which they argue that if the companies and "big unions" can join forces to squelch the protest of one small group of workers, they can also do so for other groups in the community. The strikers may also argue that the issue shows how local people are being overrun by external interests, through suggesting that the companies, unions, and perhaps the National Labor Relations Board are creatures of Washington or New York which are not responsive to local concerns.

Rhetoric and other strategies used in these situations are not always as consistent, well documented, or timely as a dispassionate observer might expect them to be. The protest group may lack organizational effectiveness, particularly in the early stages, and it will ordinarily seek to organize more effectively and perhaps recruit new talent as the conflict progresses. That arguments by participants are not always effective in particular cases is illustrated by the power-line controversy. In early stages of that conflict, slogans on leaflets and picket signs emphasized the contention that the line would carry electricity primarily for urban areas. Picket signs in summer of 1975 asked why farmers should put up with ugly towers and dangerous power lines to operate microwave ovens and color television sets in Minneapolis. Later, a statewide opinion poll indicated strong sympathy for the farmers' cause, among metropolitan residents as well as in the state generally. Subsequently, several power-line protest leaders cautioned against making metropolitan area residents the target of the protest, expressing the fear of losing the big-city support they already had. By 1977, the antiurban tone of the protests was muted considerably and was replaced eventually by arguments against the principle of eminent domain, by which utilities and other agencies can condemn private property and claim it for a public need. Opposition to eminent domain proceedings is an argument with appeal to a broad segment of the population, given the general value placed on ownership of private porperty.[3] The initial strategies leaned heavily on appeals to local interest groups; the later ones were geared to the more universal concerns and ideals of the larger social system.

KNOWLEDGE GAPS AND ORGANIZATIONAL STRATEGY

The occurrence of knowledge gaps in the social system is a phenomenon not of individual behavior but of the group process, and is therefore highly relevant to the question of strategies which groups may employ to advance their collective interests. Familiarity with arguments in controversies, and identification of the use of arguments by different groups, is a vital aspect of knowledge on public affairs topics. Even with the most esoteric public questions, the knowledge held and gained by specialists in that area will often center around potential points of debate. To illustrate: A member of the cosmopolitan elite in a community may, as part of that elite role, follow reports of the state legislature closely and be familiar with a wide range of state statutes regarding, say, elementary and high school education. That person might readily comprehend a brief report about a new development on that topic, such as a report about a change in the equalization formula of the state school-aid law. This cosmopolite may anticipate arguments for or against that law from educators and school board members in different kinds of districts, quickly perceiving potential losses to some areas and gains in others. Such perceptions of facts and insights constitute knowledge which further enhances the power of that role within a local elite group, and strengthening such roles translates into increased power for the group in which the role exists. This power may become apparent if the local community school board gets into a controversy which pits the community against the state education department over interpretation and/or application of the school-aid formula. In such a controversy, survival of the local district may be at stake and the ensuing intensity may lead to a variety of communication patterns that reduces the magnitude of the initial knowledge gap on the topic within the local community.

Existence of knowledge gaps is not necessarily dysfunctional for attainment of such social goals as community development. The cosmopolitan elites in the community with specialized interests in public affairs may be expected to have higher levels of knowledge which lead to knowledge gaps between them and other groups in the community. During times of conflict, elite groups may serve as vital community resources if the school-aid question does become a local issue. In fact, existence of knowledge elites may serve to alert the rest of the community to the relevance of the legislation to local interests and thereby create initial awareness. These knowledge elite groups may then provide information for local dissemination and discussion in a conflict setting that may tend to level differences while buttressing arguments for local interests. This is a matter not of altruism among these groups, but of maintenance of power of vested interests, which is protected by coming to the aid of the community structure. The manner and extent to which elite groups will provide their specialized information to the community at large would be expected to vary according to community structural characteristics. For example, widespread distribution of elite information would theoretically be most likely to occur in a homogeneous system in which the vested interests of the elites coincide with that of the community as a whole, compared with a more pluralistic system in which there are different elite groups with differential interests, all of which use their specialized knowledge as a resource in protecting their particular group power status.

Another question about the knowledge gap phenomenon is whether new and more specialized forms of information technology will also tend to widen gaps. A hypothesis which may be offered for future study is that technologies which are organized so as to increase the degree of differential selection of information among groups will increase the disparity in information between the have and have not groups in society. One would also expect such employment of technologies to lead to knowledge gaps on more topics, since these technologies typically are structured to provide information to specialized groups. Such outcomes would be predicted, not because of inherent characteristics of the technologies themselves but because of the structural conditions that lead to the introduction and organized use of those technologies. Specialized magazines are developed to serve publics and interests that already exist. Cable television has been promoted in some communities as a means for informing a wide range of citizens about community topics, in others as a means of providing highly specialized information to special interest groups. The latter outcome is more likely to occur, however, considering the nature of broadcast systems. In radio broadcasting, for example, the increased number of stations with specialized programming would be expected to contribute to increasing differentials in knowledge particularly in the entertainment area, among different groups, to which the stations direct their differential appeals.

INFORMATION, EDUCATION, AND ATTITUDES

A final generalization of the analysis is that opinions and knowledge may be related, but not in the simple and direct way that many observers suggest. Again, the existence of conflict appears to be a central variable. There is little evidence to support the contention that the more people know about a particular course of action being advocated by some group, the more they will support it. Any time there is a dispute within the system, the dispute is a result of vested interests, and the groups use information and knowledge as a source of support for their interests. Data from the community analyses indicate that where there is a high degree of group organization and the groups are locked in some form of contest, support for a particular course of action will show an especially weak correlation with level of knowledge and with level of education. The intensity of a community conflict appears to reduce the likelihood that individual points of view can be predicted from their educational status or from their levels of knowledge. As a conflict develops, the highly educated individuals become more likely to turn to their vested interests and to the question of whose ox is being gored as a basis for action.

STRUCTURE AND MICROPROCESSES: SOME RESEARCH DIRECTIONS

As many of the findings and interpretations of this research imply, there is a need for more systematic understanding of the microprocesses in conflict situations. These are the group and organizational processes which analytically may be treated as intervening variables between structural characteristics and knowledge and opinion outcomes in a community. These include the uses of conflict strategies, the ways in which courses of action are chosen and implemented, and—critical for the field of mass communication—the role of mass communication media in these strategies.

Literature and evidence reviewed earlier support the conclusion that media reporting of public affairs is predominantly, if not entirely, a response to social power configurations and acts of socially powerful elements within the system. This much is as true of the national "elite press" as it is of the small-town weekly newspaper or radio station. There is less known from systematic research about the processes that lead to these media reports, although several writers such as Sigal (1973) and Dunn (1969) stress the view of the press as a bureaucratic organization with specifiable linkages to other bureaucracies. The nature of these linkages have been explored in a number of case studies (Cater, 1964; Gieber, 1964; Cohen, 1963) and books about individual newspapers and experiences.

A few illustrative research questions about these microprocesses may be suggested. One such question has to do with the

specifics of interdependence between the media and the organized groups in a system. To what extent, for example, do
conflict groups depend upon media reports for information
which they will use in making later decisions about organizational strategy? Is dependence upon the media for initial reports
inversely related to the level of power of the group at that
particular point? It might be hypothesized that dependence of
all groups on media for new information is different in more
pluralistic structures, and that interactions directed toward controlling that information will be more frequent. Given the larger
number of groupings in a large and pluralistic urbanized structure, it is not possible for full exchanges of information and
ideas to occur on the primary or the secondary level. Media
reports are essential to group activity and are followed regularly. At the same time, reporters and editors who interact with
their sources in the more pluralistic system posses far more
information than their newspaper reports contain, and this
unreported information, which may or may not be verifiable,
can be exchanged in various ways. These exchanges, and their
significance for the development of conflict strategies, appear to
merit further research. Indeed, there is the question of "advocacy" versus "objective" reporting by reporters, and whether a
particular choice between these modes is made consciously or
not. If a reporter is a member of a subsystem which has a
particular vested interest, one would not expect that reporter to
treat information relevant to those interests with a relatively
high degree of objectivity. For example, journalists with specialized expertise and specialized roles in reporting medicine,
business, performing arts, or sports would not be expected to be
as neutral in their reporting of those areas as reporters who do
not have such direct ties to those areas.

Another question relates directly to media event strategies
and new media technologies. The potential importance of television for social protest is clear, given the combined audio and
visual appeal of television, which is especially geared to reporting confrontations and concerns in ways that print or radio are
unable to do. A leathery-skinned, sweating truck driver on the

picket line speaking in the local rural vernacular might be far more credible to his own group on the television screen than when quoted in print. Effectiveness with the larger viewing public, however, may be another matter. Media technologies do not alter the nature of the dispute, but are utilized according to the nature of the structure in which they exist. A tentative hypothesis is that in extended social conflicts, media event strategies go through stages of experimentation and routinization, the extent of each depending upon the resources which the countervailing groups can marshal. This means that experimentation will be more extensive in those structures that provide the widest range of resources for the organizations and the greatest diversity in media.

Media event strategies, furthermore, are often geared specifically to the linkages among different media, including the known tendencies of newspapers to write or comment about other newspapers or other media. A strategy may be designed to achieve coverage in one medium which may stimulate coverage in other media, thereby creating a bandwagon effect in which no newspaper or station wants to be left out. The case of organized farmers convincing metropolitan television stations to cover their confrontation with a county board is a case in point. When the television camera crews arrived and provided taped footage for the evening news, it was a signal to editors of local papers that this was a big story and one which local groups could not accuse them of instigating or "blowing out of proportion." On the national level, an illustrative case is Seymour Hersh's report of the My Lai massacre in Vietnam, which several prominent publications refused to use until it was carried by a number of newspapers that subscribed to a news service that used the account. Shortly after that news service report was issued, the allegations became major news in all major media.

"Experimentation" in conflict strategies is a process in which media take part, no matter how much they may try or claim to avoid it. If a picket line is ignored by a television program director who says it's "old news," the picketing group may decide they have failed one test. They may then seek from their own midst, or from without, specialized advice on what to try next and how to try it.

There is also the question of choices of media strategies according to organizational judgments of their short-run and long-run impact. The National Farmers Organization in the 1960s captured widespread attention by slaughtering farm animals before television cameras, as a protest against low farm prices. The American Agricultural Movement received widespread attention to its "tractorcade" demonstrations in Washington, D.C. These strategies themselves invariably became focal points at issue and there is usually strong pressure from inside and outside the organizations to drop these so-called radical approaches. How are these judgments made? Organizations appear to become more conservative in tactics as they widen their organizational base and deal with concerns on a regional or national level rather than with the immediate concerns of local groups.

The assumption that media communication is part of the social control process is as old as the media themselves.[4] The theatre, the printing press, the cinema, radio, and television were all introduced in an atmosphere of ideological debate about what they should and should not communicate and how they might aid in development of better citizens. Revolutions and social upheavals invariably involve the media, as do processes of more gradual change. That fact is not in doubt. What is needed is a more systematic analysis of the role of media in the process of communication and social control under varying conditions of social organization.

NOTES

1. The very fact that editorial organizations in many states have advocated and lobbied for "open meeting laws" to force local governmental bodies to admit the press and other members of the public to meetings testifies to the rigidity of decision-making procedures in various community structures. Seeking a solution through state or national legislation is often evidence of structural resistance in communities to achievement of outcomes desired by various interest groups.

2. Shortly before this writing, a major midwestern daily newspaper, as part of an extensive reshaping of its news and feature content, dropped the daily reporting of "box scores" in professional sports. After a brief period of omitting these figures, the editors announced on the front page that the omission was now considered to have been a mistake and that numerous calls and letters supposedly from readers had convinced the paper to resume the box score reports.

3. Shifting of arguments from safety and health considerations to the principle of eminent domain was cited by at least one editorial that challenged the legitimacy of the protests for that very reason. The editorial, in a regional daily newspaper that has primarily an urban readership but also circulates in the rural area where the protest occurred, pointed out that the farmers had initially objected to the line as unsafe, but later withdrew support from a proposed "Science Court" to study the merits of the safety and health concerns. The editorial did not point out that the later objections by protesters to the Science Court proposals were based partly on the belief among protesters that it would be biased in favor of the utilities.

4. For an extensive discussion of this point, see Leith (1968) on the use of different communications media during the French Revolution.

REFERENCES

BOGATY, G. A. and S. J. BALL (1971) The Second Year of Sesame Street: A Continuing Evaluation. Princeton, NJ: Education Testing Service.

BREED, W. (1958) "Mass communication and social integration." Social Forces 37: 109-116.

CATER, D. (1964) The Fourth Branch of Government. New York: Vintage.

COHEN, B. C. (1963) The Press, the Public and Foreign Policy. Princeton, NJ: Princeton University Press.

DAVIS, K., H. C. BREDEMEIER, and M. J. LEVY, Jr. (1949) Modern American Society—Readings in the Problems of Order and Change. New York: Holt, Reinhart & Winston.

DONOHUE, G. A., C. N. OLIEN, and P. J. TICHENOR (1975) "Mass media and the knowledge gap: A hypothesis reconsidered." Communication Research 2: 3-23.

DUNN, D. D. (1969) Public Officials and the Press. Reading, MA: Addison-Wesley.

GIEBER, W. (1964) "News is what newspapermen make it," pp. 173-182 in L. A. Dexter and D. M. White (eds.) People, Society and Mass Communications. New York: Macmillan.

HENNESSY, B. (1976) Public Opinion. Belmont, CA: Wadsworth.

JOHNSTONE, J.W.C. (1965) Volunteers for Learning. Chicago: AVC.

LEITH, J. A. (1968) Media and Revolution: Moulding a New Citizenry in France During the Terror. Toronto: Canadian Broadcasting Corporation.

MARTINDALE, D. and R. G. HANSON (1969) Small Town and the Nation. Westport, CT: Greenwood Press.

McLUHAN, M. (1964) Understanding Media: The Extensions of Man. New York: McGraw-Hill.

ROBINSON, J. (1967) "World affairs information and mass media exposure." Journalism Quarterly 44: 23-31.

ROLIG, N. G., J. ASCROFT, and F. WaCHEGE (1976) "The diffusion of innovations and the issue of equity in rural development." Communication Research 3: 155-169.

SHINGI, P. M. and B. MODY (1976) "The communications effects gap: a field experiment on television and agricultural ignorance in India." Communication Research 3: 171-190.

SIGAL, L. V. (1973) Reporters and Officials: The Organizations and Politics of Newsmaking. Lexington, MA: D. C. Heath.

TICHENOR, P. J., C. N. OLIEN, and G. A. DONOHUE (1970) "Mass media flow and differential growth in knowledge." Public Opinion Quarterly 34: 159-170.

VIDICH, A. J. and J. BENSMAN (1958) Small Town in Mass Society. Garden City, NY: Doubleday.

WADE, S. and W. SCHRAMM (1969) "The mass media as sources of public affairs, science and health knowledge." Public Opinion Quarterly 33: 197-209.

ABOUT THE AUTHORS

PHILLIP J. TICHENOR is Professor of Journalism and Mass Communications at the University of Minnesota. His interests include mass communication theory and methodology, mass media and public opinion, and science journalism.

GEORGE A. DONOHUE is Professor of Sociology at the University of Minnesota. His areas of specialization include social theory, socioeconomic development, and community organization.

CLARICE N. OLIEN is Professor of Rural Sociology at the University of Minnesota. Her research specialties include community organization, youth development, and mass communications.

THRESHOLD OF ETERNITY